A Beautiful Life

A Beautiful Life

THE LITTLE THINGS THAT HELP GRIEVING FAMILIES

Stedman Stevens

ISBN: 978-1-7343720-0-7

Library of Congress Control Number: 2019919891

Cover image © Nathan Anderson via Unsplash.
Cover and interior design by Katie Prince.
Typeset in Adobe Caslon Pro.

Printed by Kindle Direct Publishing.

Contents

To Ron

a remarkable person
always exemplifying grace and strength

CHAPTER I

The Call

I REMEMBER EVERYTHING ABOUT THE CALL.
It only happens once or twice in a lifetime when some event causes all five of your senses to jump into overdrive and absorb at rates that you were not aware were possible just a moment before. It was as if my eyes were open for the very first time—a truly higher level of awareness and consciousness. My internal movie camera was refreshing at twice the normal 60 GHz of the human eye and I could see and record everything with greater clarity, hue and resonance than ever before. The bright, blue fall sky outlined the green leaves at the top of the oak trees. The brackish brown of the river reflected a yellow tint of the midday sun in closely grouped ripple patterns created by the gentle breeze. Even simple thoughts took on a three-dimensional character in a way I had not known before.

It was November 4, 2005, and a sunny, brilliant Carolina day. I was sitting out on the old wooden deck overlooking the Cape Fear River, having lunch with my mom at Elijah's. It is a great restaurant, loaded with Southern specialties, seafood and the like. Sunglass clad, my mother and I talked about the good life, my great job as CEO of a division of a public company in NYC, commuting to NYC from the coast of NC, the office in Chelsea, the apartment at 52nd and 2nd, the challenges and drama of our three girls, and the fun of balancing it all.

Our move back to Wilmington, North Carolina, four months ago was a dream Lisa and I (my wife) had shared for the last two years. We'd spent the time away in Annapolis, Maryland, helping turn around a company in trouble and were glad to get back home. The town and lifestyle fit us to a T. We both loved the ocean, golf, tennis, and the slow pace Wilmington offered.

When we first moved here in 1992, we were relocating with a company from New York. I was nervous about coming back home 20 miles from where I was born. Being in NYC for seven years and Washington, DC, for four years had planted in me a seed of discomfort about the return to eastern North Carolina. I was nervous about three things, two of which I found silly:

1) I am a Southerner by birth, but have changed a fair bit by living in two large, very diverse international towns, so will it seem too slow, narrow, and constraining?

2) I love the ocean and outdoor sports, so I was going to have to practice restraint to avoid getting too much sun, as I was scared of getting skin cancer, and

3) my father gave me many great traits including resilience and optimism, but my weakness was BBQ and fried foods, not the best combination when you have a cardiovascular problem and live in the South.

We made the move returning to my hometown and it turned out well. We found a great, welcoming community and we were a typical active family. As we became more secure, we bought better toys for the kids, a bigger house, joined a beach club, a golf club, had boys' golf weekends in Pinehurst, girls' weekends in Charleston, took the kids to Disney, NYC, Washington, DC, and always had fun. Everyone in our peer group was doing the same thing: working, dance recitals, soccer, baseball, swim meets, supper clubs, and birthday parties. All along the journey, our theme song was the Rolling Stones "You Can't Always Get What You Want." We all sang it out loud every time we drove over the draw bridge at Wrightsville Beach heading for ocean fun.

Life was fairly easy with the usual suspects providing sandspurs, resistance and static. The major challenges at the time ranged from a tough business customer, an employee problem at work, a rough start at school for one of the girls, some political issues in the community, what to renovate around the house, when to replace the cars, vacation trips with the family, Christmas presents for three growing girls, and more. We were enjoying a good life.

My wife, Lisa, was outgoing with an infectious laugh that came easily. She was welcoming to everyone. When she asked people questions, she listened to the answers. Her hazel eyes and playful demeanor made her an instant hit with guys of all ages. Her willingness to listen and patience built strong female friendships. She was always ready to dance. The children still remember all of us dancing in the kitchen to "Be Young Be Foolish Be Happy" by The Tams. We would dance in the grocery store, on the beach and just about anywhere. We were happy and together we were living the good life with few bumps in the road.

While doing most of the usual married and family things, Lisa and I also consciously did something very different. Most people we met thought we were the happiest people on the planet. Our happiness was driven by our being like-minded partners who openly talked things through, always clearing the deck before going to sleep. What we did a bit differently was that we actively engaged and welcomed our friends into our life, openly and transparently. With an open mindset and flexibility of topics we would discuss things with our friends that appeared to be impeding their happiness. We usually started off the discussion by sharing one of our challenges and posing a question to the group about how they handled similar experiences. It may sound a bit intrusive, but it was the opposite of shallow cocktail chatter. Our discussions were usually on a narrow topic, but deep in exploring the core composite of feelings or beliefs. By nature, we were very active, highly social, and sought out the good parts of life, all while navigating obstacles thrown our way. We invited lively discussions and arguments about cultures, travel, politics (but not about people), how to make our world a better place, and what we were doing to fulfill that desire. Our parties were a safe place that allowed each person to be and express themselves.

Perhaps our work experiences in DC and New York made it easier for us to seamlessly fit into most social and business environments. While doing all of the usual things, we also had great opportunities to do unusual things. We were invited to a New Year's Eve ball in Vienna by an Austrian business executive and were Austrian for a night without a glitch. We traveled the world to open new business opportunities and to satisfy my itch for international business. On a US Department of Commerce trade mission, we met Shirley Temple Black when she was an ambassador to Czechoslovakia. We visited good friends who won governor, Senate, and House of Representative seats in several states. As the USSR was breaking apart, I traveled to the Republic of Georgia, meeting the president, prime minister, and senior ministers of the country, looking to acquire and grow businesses in America. I had the naïve idea that I could possibly be a mini Armand Hammer by tapping into one of the greatest political transitions in history and building consolidated food companies from the fragmented Soviet hangover.

The emerging Russian powers had other ideas.

One night, I sat at dinner with a Russian vodka manufacturer who was considering helping us import and export products. He had one or two shots too many and started explaining how the United States was more corrupt than Russia. I expressed a conciliatory view that both countries struggle with this problem. "Careful," said my interpreter, keeping her smile fixed on her face. She worked for the KGB in her day job. "You should agree, as he can have you killed in an instant." I told the man I agreed with him. Later that month, five bank executives in Moscow were mysteriously killed. It was my last trip to Russia.

Back home, our active social life continued. Lisa founded an annual "Hot Moms in the Hood" party for all the neighborhood women. It was three hours of champagne, mimosas, and loud talking from 10:00 a.m. to 1:00 p.m. Everyone could be themselves without any label, prerequisites or requirements. It was a fantastic celebration of women and moms.

We were very comfortable with our life, our family, and ourselves. The good life. But "life is good" and a thousand other clichés were about to evaporate before me, like dry ice in the summer sun.

My mom and I were just finishing our lunch on that great sunny day, when a call from my good friend changed everything.

Jack is a great internal medicine specialist and like me, an erratic golfer. He had seen my wife earlier in the day for an ultrasound for a persistent stomach pain. We joked that she must have an ulcer from living with me and should return to working a regular job, since raising three girls was so much more stressful. But earlier in the day he did not like the way the ultrasound looked, foggy and inconclusive. As a Forensic Scientist and in the business of educating Physicians, I was informed just enough to be nervous. Upon prodding, he thought there were masses, and some were large. An MRI would clear up the questions.

It did.

The wind blowing into my Motorola clam shell cell phone and the loud noise of a table beside us just getting their food made it a bit hard to hear. I strained and asked him to repeat what he said. He tried to explain that she had masses in her liver of varying sizes. It was hard to tell how functionality had been affected. He continued on for ten minutes regurgitating his knowledge and substantial experience, stumbling around his words, before I finally asked him outright. I knew him well enough to know when he was hiding.

"Jack, what is the deal?"

He started slowly, methodically. "She has a dozen masses, some greater than two centimeters, making them inoperable. Her liver looks like a bag of golf balls and is functioning below 50 percent capacity. She has the MRI of an 80-year-old, late stage cancer patient."

"Which cancer?"

"Not sure, but most likely pancreatic. It is difficult to tell sometimes where it starts, where it goes and what is going on."

"Okay, pancreatic cancer. But what does that mean? What is the prognosis? How long? One year, five years, and how many surgeries will it take to extend her life?" His voice tightened up and he became more direct. Unbeknownst to me, he was putting on his professional armor to protect himself; he needed to make it professional and deal with the personal aspects by himself. I was still trying to process which cancer, as I did not know anything about pancreatic cancer or what it meant for a treatment regimen. I totally missed the significance of inoperable tumors in the liver. My mind was racing with things to do, colleagues to call, doctors to see. My good friend, who just happened to be my physician, struggled bringing clarity to my questions.

Physicians by their nature and choice of occupation are a competitive bunch, not fond of defeat. The broad nature of diseases makes it more difficult for patients and families to get accurate information that is helpful in developing a plan of action for the family. Running a medical education company, I learned that a physician talking about not being able to save a patient is rare. It is just not a situation that they are effectively trained or willing to accept. The silence and pain on the other end of the telephone was like taking a deep breath of air in minus ten-degree weather. It became increasingly obvious. He could not even squeak it out.

"Jack, help me with some context here," I said. "What are we facing? What and how long?" Jack hemmed and hawed for a few minutes and then spit out the answer that was bone crushingly clear. "Your wife has days, but not years to live. Likely weeks, but not months."

He was right—it was forty-two days.

CHAPTER II

What Do We Do Now?

WHERE DO YOU GO FROM RECEIVING THE NEWS that your wife of twenty-two and a half years, mother of your three beautiful daughters, is going to die, and soon?

So started a tortuous, excruciating journey. This book started with the intention of chronicling a story for my girls, who may not have captured all the texture of the scene that was being painted around them at nine, twelve, and fifteen years old. This work has evolved from a story for my three daughters to a message that others might benefit from.

A Beautiful Life travels over a ten-year family journey through grief, anxiety, depression, eating disorders, and severe mental health issues, equipping the reader with unique tools to support a grieving family. Our family hopes this work will help the families, friends, and relatives of an affected family participate in a positive, nurturing approach to supporting a grieving family wrestling with emotional intensity. We also seek to assemble thoughts that expand the grieving family's ability to cope with the extraordinary challenge they are facing.

We hope this book uniquely provides experiences and learnings to address the enormous informational void relating to the emotions of grieving children, families, and friends.

The highest goal of this work would be to lighten the burden placed on grieving families and friends, particularly on young children. We hope our experiences help others get through the agonizing transition between what your life was yesterday, what it is today, and what it will be tomorrow. Quite simply, your life is never the same. The instant it changes, you must start to process the change, accept some part of it, and start reconciling the rest of your life plan.

Be present.

Our hope is that friends of grieving people will learn from these thoughts and perhaps help their friends and themselves deal with the trauma of grief. Frankly, if your friend is grieving, it is important that you focus on their needs and put your needs, wants, and thoughts in the back of the emotional bus. They cannot support you as they have in the past, nor can they shoulder your grief load. For the health of your grieving friends, you must focus on the needs of the front-line grievers. Even as a close friend of the family, it is crucial to subordinate your grief process to the family's burden, which is greater. Grief affects people outside of the family life for a small period of time each week, perhaps only an hour or so, whereas it affects the direct family every minute of every day and for the rest of their lives.

The message is simple: Even with the most unthinkable loss, there is hope and the future is bright, even in the darkest hour you can live—A Beautiful Life.

As we go forward walking through the years, grasping to understand how the call at 1:30 p.m. on November 4, 2005, affected our family, relatives, and friends' lives for years, consider the benefit of understanding the connection of this and other distant points in time. Is there something to be learned from these experiences that may be applied to other situations along the way? How did I not see the ten years of a boiling emotional pot leading to a confluence of events that erupted into an emergency room?

CHAPTER III

How Do You Tell Your Daughters that Their Mom Is Going to Die, and Soon?

MY DYING WIFE AND I STRUCK OUT on our journey to prepare, protect, and parent our three sweet innocent daughters. There is no right or wrong way to convey this message, but there may be a better or worse way to help your children transition through one of the most difficult experiences of their young lives. Oddly, we did not feel the enormity of the task we were undertaking at the time, probably due to stress, fatigue, and emotional exhaustion, but we both felt there was a very important mission to accomplish that would affect our children's lives for decades. We developed a plan and set out to talk to our teenage girls about their mother's health and to tell them she was going to die.

We decided that it might go better if Dad walked them through this forest alone as the immediate emotional intensity of a sick parent in the room would make it harder for them to ask open questions. I thought of all the times we did Daughters-and-Dad-Only-Days, giving Mom a break for the weekend. Planting flowers every year, building things with hammers and saws, renting a convertible, picking out artwork together, and ten-year-old birthday trips. Little did I know that along those fun journeys, I was laying the bedrock of our relationship for this most difficult period of my three daughters' lives.

We decided that a strong footing on which to build this bridge was honest and timely communication. That is, be honest with your children, omitting some of the granular, gory details, but tell them. Tell them what you know when you know it and tell them what you don't know. Having read as much as possible in three days about processing grief and how children of different ages perceived it, I felt a bit humbled by what I did not know.

Tell them what you know in the same time frame as you learn it, because they already know something is up. In the span of 42 days from diagnosis to death and unsure of the time frame, we broke our communication with our children into four segments. That might sound cold or callous, but we knew time was short, and it was the best chance we had to prepare them for the rest of their lives.

Within days of really understanding what we thought was going on, we started the process of informing our girls that their mom was going to die. We learned new things daily. We focused our best thinking on keeping the girls informed with what we knew almost each day as it changed. Mind you, I thought I would throw up blood every step of the way and with each conversation with my daughters, but we needed to give them information in bites that we knew were true and thought, at the time, they'd be able to understand.

The discussion with the girls went like this:

THE FIRST WEEK

"Your mom is sick, and we do not know what it is," because we really did not know which cancer and what the prognosis window was. We did know it was serious and likely fatal, but like many before us, we found ourselves thinking, *Well, breast cancer has a pretty good five-year survival rate, so we can work through the issues.* After my readings, I thought I knew what the likely outcome was, but still wanted to be sure and hear from our oncologists.

THE SECOND WEEK

"Your mom has cancer, and we do not know how we will treat it."
The big "C" is a showstopper for all ages. Everyone has some perception that cancer is a really bad thing to have, and many people
do not recover from it. The white elephant was in the room. Everyone was uncomfortable and no one knew what to say.

The perplexing thing for the physicians about her cancer was
that her blood test results did not match the tissue biopsies. The
doctors explained that it was difficult to discern which cancer was
prevalent and therefore which to treat first. Inertia is very difficult
for me, so I ungraciously suggested that waiting to figure out a correct diagnosis was unlikely to produce a good outcome, and that we
were sacrificing time for accuracy. My wife chose the recommended treatment regimen.

THE THIRD WEEK

"Your mom has cancer and is going to die." This was hard to say
and harder for the children to hear. Fear and anxiety naturally ran
rampant.

"What do you mean? How is that possible? Why is this happening? What did I do to deserve this? What did I do to cause this?"

There was not a lot of discussion or explaining, just discomfort
and dismay.

"What do we do now?"

I did not have the answers.

THE FOURTH WEEK

"Your mom has cancer and is going to die in the next few weeks."
At this point, these beautiful innocent teenage girls were shell-
shocked. It was just not within their grasp of anything they had
faced or even comprehended in their life thus far.

Communicating in this manner turned out to be very important, because children need time to process that which they do not understand. Death is a foreign concept to most teenagers. We all need time to digest things. Four weeks is not enough time to digest a 200-pound gorilla of information, but we thought we must do it for their sakes, while their mother was still alive.

As each week passed, the girls would get up, get dressed, and go to school. I cooked breakfast as always and sometimes it seemed as if it was not real. It was surely a dream, right? The smiling, laughing, rambunctious household of the past was now silent. It was one of the first times I could clearly hear footsteps in the house. And I could hear the quiet, shuffled footsteps of someone hanging on to life by a thread.

No path for grieving is better than the other. Whatever feels most natural to you is the correct answer. Children, on the other hand, seem more influenced by their age and maturity. There was a definite spread in understanding—actions and reactions—between nine, twelve, and fifteen years old.

My experience is that children live in their own world. We think they live in ours, but they just humor us.

As the girls took in the news, Piaget's developmental theories seemed to play out in front of my eyes. His cognitive development stages involve changes in thought processes and the ability to process actions and events. Could it be that grief follows similar developmental patterns? Under normal life circumstances, a child is developmentally different at nine, twelve, and fifteen years old. How does a sudden and traumatic event affect this normal developmental period? Retrospectively, I would have made it clearer to each girl that no matter what happened, we were going to be okay, and that they were going to be okay, too. I did not understand how worried they were that everything was about to change: their home, their school, their clothes, and everything else they might've feared. I regret not attending to this fear with greater care.

Three sisters with three years of age differences are worlds apart.

A nine-year-old still lives in a fantasy land dominated by dolls, pretend friends, and television shows. The line defining reality and make believe has yet to be informed by real life events. A twelve-year-old is becoming hyperaware of the pressures of middle school and not much else. It is such an emotional and physical period of transition. It shows every day in its intensity: all things are of paramount importance, and adults just don't understand. A fifteen-year-old is acutely aware of emerging adulthood: social challenges of friends, school, and families. While digesting and participating in the beginning stages of young adulthood, teenagers will often have an occasional pang for simplicity, for returning to playing with dolls in the quiet made up world which she controls.

Perhaps a sudden significant trauma effects that developmental bridge, hindering or blocking the transition and expected development. Could it be that a child is marooned on the bridge by a life changing event? How is it that some continue to develop, some change developmental pace, and some just do not move forward? I wish I had the answers.

CHAPTER IV

Grief Therapy

IT WAS A BIT UNCOMFORTABLE talking with the girls about what we did and did not know about their mother's condition, because they already knew things in their life were rapidly changing. But it is extremely important to explain and define what you know and that some things are unknown. Children will hold you accountable for everything you tell them during this traumatic time. Transparently letting them know what is not known will help you and them in the distant future. Comforting comments like, "She will be okay" (some friends said to the girls) are not helpful, and they will remember, ten years later, who told them the big lie. These well-meaning comments seem to germinate a seed of resentment and anger in the future. This reinforces the need for parental transparency and discussing with your grieving children that people mean well and may not say things that are helpful.

We are all unique. We all think differently. We all seek out different things in life. We all hear, talk, and act differently. It seems natural that we all might grieve differently, too. Of all the books and articles I read, Lieberman's thinking is the most consistent with my experience and understanding of grief processing and pace.

There seem to be four categories of grief processing. One grief pattern is "anticipatory," or early, grieving. It starts before the event with moderate to intense grief that decreases to mild experiences of pain within a year. A second style could be called "prolonged." These grievers show moderate to intense grief for a year and beyond. A third is "delayed" grievers, who show little or no grief in the first few years, with emotions surfacing years later. The last group are "sharp" grievers. They show immediate and intense grief for a very short period of time, and almost no grief at the one-year mark. Therapy can help you understand how you grieve and provide tools for success. It seems I am a combination of an anticipatory griever before the event, and a sharp griever after the event.

Talk therapy is an option you are either open-minded about or not. There aren't many fence-sitters on this topic. Our family's experience with grief therapy is a bit mixed. It seems that age and personality have a lot to do with how engaged a person is in talk therapy. I was very open to therapy, as I have always been intrigued about why people think and act the way they do. That is, the social behavior behind actions was always interesting to me: why people buy certain brands of clothes or cars, preferences in food types, thick spaghetti sauce or thin, etc. It seems many adults have a closed mind and are not as open to therapy, representing a protective shell or fear of what may be discovered.

If you find that your first experience with therapy is not helpful, you may not have found a therapist who is a good personal match for you. Do not stop searching. The process can be immensely helpful with the right person and environment.

My oldest daughter embraced the potential benefits of therapy as well and cheerfully went through the exercises. Several years later, once she was in college, she joined a grief group for additional support and had a roommate who had lost her mom as well. They are still close friends. My middle daughter participated but was skeptical. She wears her emotions on her sleeve, and it is obvious when she is in pain. She thought she did not need help feeling and expressing her emotions. My youngest totally refused to engage in therapy. She gave us all the stiff arm any time we said let's talk.

Grief counseling was a good idea for all of us, although one of us did not engage. Weeks before their mom's passing, hospice recommended a session with me and the three girls. We sat in a room together and talked about feelings, about what an emotion is and why we have them. Parts of the discussion exposed raw nerves and sadness, while some provided soothing salve at the same time. During one session, the counselor presented a clay pot to each of us. She asked us to take them home with us, and to come back next week with ideas for all of the feelings we would like to put in the pot, feelings that reminded us of Lisa. Feelings that would honor her. The following week, the four of us showed up with our clay pots. She asked us to list two feelings, one happy and one sad, and put them in the pot. I started with my great happiness and thankfulness for the three daughters Lisa had given us. My sadness was not having her there to see her daughters grow up. Charlotte was happy that her mom was so outgoing, and sad that her mom talked on the cell phone in the car when they were driving around, taking time away from talking with her daughter. June was happy that we had so many fun days on the beach together, and sad that her mom was not going to be there for more fun times. We felt soothed by this exercise, and could see many more emotions and feelings being added to the clay pot for safekeeping. Rose looked at the pot intensely, as if she was trying to make it explode with X-ray vision. She focused on the pot and did not say anything.

The therapist said, "Rose, tell us about the feelings you would like to put in your pot?"

She slowly and calmly replied, "I do not have any feelings to put into the pot."

"We all have feelings. What is in your pot?"

"Nothing."

"Rose, it cannot be nothing. You have feelings and emotions about your mom, and it is very natural that you would want to share some of them with us." She said she did not have any feelings to put in the pot and that she was the unlucky one because she had the least time with her mom.

So it went then, and so it goes today.

In an unusual way, this nine-year-old girl was locked up. She repressed her emotions in order to feel nothing. Various therapists and psychiatrists tried in vain to get her to open up, but with no luck.

Therapy was also helpful for me after Lisa's passing to help squash the negative internal chatterbox on my left shoulder, while helping my positive right shoulder speak up. The left chatterbox would say, "You told the children too fast, no, too slow, not using the right words, not giving them time to take in what was happening to them. You should have asked others for more help, you should not have let them have sleepovers away from the house during that last week when you knew she would pass and they would need to see her, no, they would have been more traumatized to see their mother dead in their living room," and on and on and on.

The right chatterbox was much quieter, gently reminding me, "You were nose-to-nose with your partner of twenty-three years every minute of every day for forty-two days. You did it right. You told the girls in the most compassionate way possible. You did the best you could possibly have done with what you had."

Therapy cleared my head and extracted the poison at the same time. It gave me mental tools and techniques to deal with emotions that were unfamiliar and venomous. Some of the tools included recognizing the negative chatter and pausing it sooner, or replacing it with positive thoughts. It became progressively easier to recognize the negative earlier on and cutting it off at the start, replacing the negative thought with a positive one. I learned to clear my mind and just listen to whatever thought popped into my head. Many times, it was a positive memory of my wife which always elicited a smile from me. Sometimes it even felt as if she was communicating with me. Emotional energy like that felt like a warm blanket on a cold rainy day, and was tremendously soothing and calming during this difficult emotional transition. That memory and my response to it would tell me: It is going to be okay; it is going to be okay. Therapy also helped me manage the grief triggers that came up daily (which I will discuss later). An experienced therapist can provide simple means for you to regain control of your emotional roller coaster and reel it in, in bounds.

CHAPTER V

Understanding the Relationship of Grace, Graciousness, Gratitude, Empathy, and Sympathy

SOMETIMES IT IS HARD TO PARSE WORDS or even understand the slight or fine difference in meanings, but these three words came to mean something very different to me. Grace (noun) is mostly associated with a station in life or position or courtesy, generosity or a favor. Some people live it as a lifestyle. Others do not even comprehend it. During our odyssey, we were the beneficiaries of many gracious acts. One of the greatest gifts you can give to a grieving friend is the gift of graciousness.

Graciousness (adjective) is an elegant, magnanimous, compassionate gift of benevolence laden with kindness, thoughtfulness, good intentions and courtesy. It is an action, an attitude that makes everyone feel welcomed. Being gracious can take on many forms, such as giving someone the benefit of the doubt for actions that were not what you had hoped for, or allowing extra room in a discussion. Simply providing someone with more padding under their mental carpet by giving them a compliment or a pat on the back will go a long way. All in all, graciousness is a gift that we all have within us, but are slow to recognize, and hesitant to give away. The price of grace is the expense of our ego, ambition, avarice, want, and desire. It is the antimatter to much of the hate, anger, and deceit we tolerate in the world today.

Being gracious, or depositing grace in the empty vault of a friend in need, pays off in multitudes. Share it freely and frequently. It is not hard, but does require focus and persistence. However, it is a great thing to share, water, grow, and expand. Reach inside and think about others: their plights, desires, problems, limitations, challenges, and needs. No gift of graciousness is too small. A thoughtful note, card, or gift will help boost someone in a time of need. A book you thought might help them, washing their car, offering to pick something up at the store or dry cleaners—all can be great gifts to someone in emotional need.

Gratitude (noun) is an appreciative acknowledgment of someone's efforts. "Thank you for those kind words, I appreciate what you did," and others. It seems easy to dispense, but hard to find. Gratitude seems to be more about the giver, while graciousness is about the recipient.

Empathy in conjunction with sympathy in the grief process are often confused by the giver and the receiver. Both are important in their appropriate place. Empathy is truly about the grieving person. You can feel the pain they are suffering and look around the room at the situation with compassion and understanding. Sympathy is trickier. It is about both the giver showing respect, appropriateness, and sharing feelings, while the recipient feels relief, acknowledgment, and validation. Without being too cynical, it feels as though sympathy in today's society is more of a social standard, focused more on the words and form than truly conveying an emotional investment to a friend. Or maybe we just don't know how to express the emotions we are feeling.

A colleague at one of the top healthcare centers in the US facilitated a quick appointment with a team of cancer experts. We were fortunate with a few calls to secure the right appointments and were fast tracked into the right department, which is hard for anyone, even at a local hospital, so I felt lucky. In less than a week, we walked into the exam room and the two physicians briefly interviewed us with smiles and handshakes, asking about the politics of how we got the appointment. The physicians diligently focused on asking specific questions about diet, lifestyle, preferences, and habits. Then they exited the room to go next door to review the lab tests and build a strategy.

They quickly returned, ashen faced and no smiles. Speaking slowly and deliberately, they explained that the cancer was extremely advanced in several organs of the body. While she looked like a healthy forty-six-year-old on the outside, her internal organs looked like that of a ninety-year-old with terminal cancer. We were stunned and tried to process what we had heard. No surgery, no treatment, no options, nowhere to go—except home.

We flew home that afternoon, arriving just before sunset. South Live Oak Drive is one of the oldest streets in this 250-year-old Southern town. The street gets its name from the 118 live oaks that line each side of the road for almost a mile and a half. It is an iconic picture. Each beautiful tree is over 150 years old with arms reaching out left and right, hanging low, forming a canopy over the road. Growing low and long, live oaks are covered all year by robust green leaves shaped like thin bananas. For a decade, I jogged up and down the street for exercise four times a week. It was therapeutic, calming—relaxing karma. It is a familiar and heartwarming street for me.

My wife and I returned from Sloan Kettering Cancer Center, traveling the usual path home. But that day, the quiet street steeped in history delivered one of the greatest expressions of grace and gratitude I've ever experienced.

Upon returning from Sloan Kettering, friends had tied large white bows on the 118 live oak trees on South Live Oak Drive, knowing we'd see them on our drive home from the airport. It showed us they were hopeful, but also seemed to say that they knew our results.

To this day, I do not know who authored the braided confluence of grace, gratitude, and graciousness.

CHAPTER VI

Hospice

SEPARATION, DIVORCE, AND DEATH OF A SPOUSE all entail a tumultuous period of transition in which everyone loses something. Statistics show that *you* are significantly more likely to end up in the hospital in the next twelve months because of your trauma. People who have been through one of these disruptive life events will likely have some understanding of the other forms of loss. These loses might include a sacred bond, perhaps a loss of trust, confidence, self-esteem, self-control, or a partner to trade the most intimate of sacred thoughts with. Children lose the richness of a family unit, the security of knowing there are two parents if something happens to one. The innocence and good life of a child passes into history in the blink of an eye; such a time of loss and certain loneliness descends upon the family like a cloud you never knew existed. It is not quantifiable or even understandable, but the discomfort can be present in the room with the exact same people where months before it was not.

Witnessing and participating in a forty-two-day death spiral from a cancer running wild is one of the most inhumane and agonizing things I have ever experienced. I suffered watching the person I had 26,280 meals with before this now not be able to eat any food. In her last ten days, my wife got pleasure from rolling barbeque pretzel bits in her mouth until the flavor was gone and then depositing the pretzel in a bowl at her bedside. Her love for great cuisine was diminished to barbecue seasoning on a pretzel. The good news was that the spices on the pretzels gave her a brief moment of pleasure in a scorning desert of pain. Her passing was the Nadir Day in our lives.

Hospice care workers step into this hurricane and provide a great service to patient and family. Their experience is crucial, their depth of understanding vast, their sense of empathy boundless, and their compassion for humanity fluently conveyed. They prepare you for the crossing of a loved one. They describe a range of what to expect.

Hospice nurses and staff were tremendously helpful, well-trained and professional. They provided guidance and support, setting up a special bed, special pillows, walkers, and aids we might not have thought of. These people came by our house every day to check medicines and offer any other support. It was calming knowing that such professionals were helping us as they had helped hundreds of others in our situation. Each worker that came into our home projected a quiet respect that was amazingly present with the situation, but not intrusive. It would have been a different and more difficult experience without them. The hospice team came into our home to help us stabilize, understand, and prepare us for the transition. From the very first call, the hospice care workers were fully engaged and tremendously respectful of our privacy and feelings. They would offer suggestions in a subtle way, and always answer our questions with sensitivity and patience. Every aspect of our life benefited from their experience. From the emotional challenges down to ordering and setting up the bed, providing walkers, back supporters, bandages, managing medications, and more.

Thank you, Lower Cape Fear Hospice, for everything.

All the medications and bandages were set up in the living room near the only lounge chair that was comfortable for Lisa to sleep. We stripped our small living room bar of scotch and vodka and replaced it with tissues, paper towels, water, and bandages. Syringes, alcohol swabs, and injectable prescriptions replaced our cocktail mixers. It was our battlefield aid station close to the patient. One afternoon my fifteen-year-old and I were home with her mom, and we needed more alcohol swabs for an injection. The drugstore was just around the corner, so I asked my oldest daughter to patient-sit for a few minutes while I ran out. She said fine as she always did, the oldest and a rule follower. I showed her the bar and everything she could need for the next few minutes while I was gone, and to call me if anything made either of them nervous. She said, "What is the yellow paper marked DNR?" I picked up the paper and walked outside with her and sat on the front porch.

I showed her the paper and slowly started talking. "Remember when I told you about the days I drove an ambulance in college? As an ambulance driver, when you arrive at an accident, you do everything humanly possible to help people and check the ABCs: Airway, Breathing, and Circulation."

"Dad, the short version please; the yellow paper," she said.

"Okay, so when I showed up to an accident scene I had to—and was required by law—to do everything I could do to help stabilize and get people to a hospital. When you are very sick like your mom, you do not always want those extraordinary methods to be tried. So, your mom signed this legal document that says Do Not Resuscitate (DNR), and we have to keep it here in plain sight so if something happens, we have it to show to the emergency personnel, police, or doctor."

I paused, and she and I both started crying slow, small tears. We were both fairly cried out over the last few weeks, but it was hard not to tear up sitting there together on our front porch. She was days away from her Sweet Sixteen. I wanted something different for her.

In many ways it seems much of my life experience was in preparation for those few weeks of helping my wife in her last days. Training as an emergency medical technician at eighteen, being an EMT, emergency room work in college, research, injections, patient care, patient education, and clinical trials... but nothing prepares you for seeing your spouse melt away day after day. Bleeding uncontrollably from her nose, mouth, ears, eyes, and every other possible place only added to the indescribable sadness, pain, and profoundness of suffering. I have never cried so much before or after those last ten days of my wife's life. Only a few days before the end, during one of the most degrading personal experiences for her, she made a profound statement.

"Dying is easy. Cleaning up the mess that this leaves will be excruciating."

It was. And it still is.

CHAPTER VII

Charlotte: A 15-Year-Old's View

MY MOM WOKE UP ONE DAY with a horrible stomachache; forty-two days later she died. Each day I watched her as she weakened with the cancer inside her growing stronger, overtaking everything I knew as my mother. Near the end her face was barely a skeleton, her skin sallow, yellow and thin; but the scariest thing was the morphine.

The morphine eased her pain but increased ours. It made her tired and her speech slurred, her eyelids would stay open, but her cloudy eyes would roll into the back of her head, her mouth dropping open, waiting for death to climb in.

Watching someone die is an experience you will never forget. I was in complete disbelief as I watched each painful step. Hope and optimism are powerful coping mechanisms. My two sisters and I banded together. Once you have seen how easily life can be taken away, you never take it for granted again. Though my younger sisters were only nine and twelve at the time, we understood each other's sadness and were there for each other whenever someone needed comforting. The bond of sisterhood helped us by coming together. We were able to cope with our sadness, anxiety, and anger toward Mom, God, and ourselves. What had we done to deserve to watch our mother die? What will Dad do? What will we do with only our dad?

Eventually, we all came to accept that it was her time to go, and that everything must happen for a reason. By making ourselves believe it was all part of some grand plan, one we would eventually come to understand someday, we were able to find a shred of solace.

Being fifteen years old versus my youngest sister at nine when our mom passed away helped me a lot. I was devastated, but I was also self-centered and in my own world with my friends. They meant everything to me, not only because of my loss, but because they became my new tribe. I couldn't explain this to Dad. He was trying to steer me away from a somewhat sketchy friend, and would say things like, "When you walk into a room together with your friend, you are all painted with the same brush. Is that the brush you want to be painted with?" I was okay with the risk of that brush. He didn't fully appreciate that relationships are the most important things teenagers have. Friends give us a needed comfort. The possibility of more change or moving after Mom's death was intense. I still feel the anxiety of my eighth grade move to Annapolis, which was only for two years, but seemed an eternity. The severing of those relationships would have been too much to bear. When you move and no longer have that support system, it takes forever to build back up. I focused on working hard in school because I knew a good college was my ticket to freedom.

Although sadness still surprises and haunts me some days, the bond with my sisters helped me get through her death and enabled me to move forward and live in the now. I hope that someday I will understand why all this happened, and more clearly understand how each of us are stronger, better people because of it.

Dad always told us that we should do our best to enjoy the age we're at. So be fifteen when you're fifteen, or a college freshman when you're a college freshman. He was also clear that no one was assuming Mom's role, that I was fifteen years old and should continue to live the life of a fifteen-year-old. We tried, but an experience like this is life-changing. It robs you of some of your childhood and matures you forever.

In those first weeks, I felt a different obligation of being the oldest with a greater burden to bear than my sisters, in addition to being a student and sister. As the oldest child, I thought it was my job to fill the gap our mom left behind, and I did the best I could to console and support my broken family. Losing a loved one is like losing a part of yourself. My mind was fuzzy, and I continually felt as if I was watching myself live life from the view of an outsider, unable to truly experience the more positive activities I was involved in, all while attempting to fill the space my mom had left behind.

CHAPTER VIII

June: A 12-Year-Old's View

AS THE MIDDLE CHILD, I'm used to getting left out and losing things. I was the cute newborn for a while, but started walking at seven months old. My older sister got all the attention while I was younger and clumsy, but I was okay with that because I was the younger sister. Then, just when I started being really cute, along came my younger sister, a baby that everyone thought was adorable. I was transformed to the middle sister. I mean, when's being the middle of anything ever good? Middle of the road, middle of the pack, middle of the grading curve, average, between, intermediate, or...?

My mom's death was the big one, the big loss. And it all happened in the middle of the seventh grade drama queens and mean girls—I lost my mom in a month. Just one month earlier I was all wrapped up in being a full blown twelve-year-old in middle school. Whispering, secret notes, and running hard with my pack. It was blissful drama.

I knew my mom's illness was bigger, longer-lasting than any of the small stuff I was dealing with, but my normal life of school and friends was right in front of me. Some friends tried to help, but no one knew what to say. What do you say? I think my good friend, Lillie, said it best.

She said, "I do not know what to say, but when you want to talk, give me a call; I will be there to listen."

It was perfect because it let me know I had a safe place to go. I had someone my own age outside of my family that I could call on my own time, whenever I was ready.

My thirteenth birthday came one month and four days after my mom died. I missed her, but Dad put on a good birthday party and my friends went out of their way to make it special. After all, I am a teenager now! Dad promised us that we'd get a cell phone on our thirteenth birthday (thank you, Charlotte, for blazing the trail). The day had finally come to get my very own cell phone! Dad picked me up before school was out and before my birthday party to go get it. I was really excited. I spent an hour looking at different phones and picked out my favorite. The representative started the paperwork, got my dad's telephone number, and looked up the account.

"Oh," she said. "You did not set up the account and are not the primary, so I need to speak with Mrs. Stevens."

I looked at Dad and he looked at me. I've never seen him afraid or scared, but he was petrified with fear. He did not speak. When she said it again, I began to cry, and Dad too. He explained to her what had happened last month and managed to get me through getting my first phone. I was happy to get my phone, but sad and angry too. Why did she have to die? Is her death going to continue to steal my happiness like it did today?

I'm still alive and she's still not here. How can I change that?

CHAPTER IX

"Mommy, Why Are You Not Going to Be at My Tenth Birthday Party?"

"MOMMY, WHY WON'T YOU BE HERE for my tenth birthday?"

Rose's question was bone crushing for us. This is a nine-year-old's nightmare. "I miss my mommy." Her other questions were equally disarming: "Why are you not here?" "What do I say when my friends ask me if my mom will let me sleep over tonight?" "What will happen to all the stuff in my room?"

I did not recognize the importance of this last question. It was slow and hard learning for me, what it was I needed to highlight that would not change in their lives, what would stay the same as before. It was an obvious question that I did not anticipate or respond to well, but required significant attention.

Rose: A 9-Year-Old's View

"I don't understand why I was so unlucky. I had the least time with Mom. Why did she have to go?" I laughed when Dad explained that Mom was sick and what was happening to her, because I really did not understand what he meant, and I was nervous. I'm still so ashamed of how I reacted. I laughed again at Mom's funeral service when our favorite Rolling Stones song, "You Can't Always Get What You Want," came on. I knew people went to sleep and did not wake up. I knew pets went away and did not come back. But my mom has always been here, and is supposed to always be here, right? I'm the child. Who will take care of me now? What will happen to the things in my room? Where will I live? Where will I go? What's next? Maybe she will come home one day soon.

I didn't know what life could be like without her. I guess I'm the least lucky as I had the shortest amount of time with her. Or maybe I'm the luckiest as I had the most time with her in the last nine years at home? I'm mad at her and her friends who took her time when she should have been playing with me. I'm mad at myself because I said I wish things were different.

But most of all I'm scared.

CHAPTER X

Talking with Your Spouse about Death: What Would We Do If…

AS MANY MARRIED COUPLES DO in twenty-four years of marital discussions, we talked about what we would want to happen in a variety of situations that we had never encountered. We both agreed that if faced with a terminal illness, we would want to know. It had been an interesting hypothetical discussion between husband and wife with a glass of wine, not really thinking it would ever happen.

Facing the reality was quite a different situation.

Thinking back to that first day of receiving the news from Jack, I remembered waiting until Lisa went to sleep and running down to my home office to get on the internet for more information and hope. That night, I looked up every clinical trial involving pancreatic cancer. I knew where to look since I had been running a clinical trial patient recruitment company; clinical trials are the leading edge of drug testing and outcome improvement.

What I learned from the current state of clinical trials investigating new drugs for pancreatic cancer was devastatingly obvious. There were not many trials in process, which meant there were not many drugs that were working effectively, but more importantly, the mid-point that designated the success of a medicine and the desired outcomes of the medicine were stated in weeks, not years. This was stunning. Many clinical trials talk about extending life expectancy, improved quality of life, adding decades of better health, or extending life for years. Not one of the current clinical trials being done in the wealthiest nation on the planet had an outcome that added one year of life to patients with this disease. Most desired outcomes were expressed in weeks. I knew what my good friend had told me was true, that my wife had only weeks to live, but as an eternal optimist I was trying to find a glimmer of hope. Hope died that night, and I cried for a half hour before going back to bed.

Little did I know, it was Nadir minus 42.

I thought for a few days about whether I should honor our prior agreement and be totally honest about her terminal illness. I put it off day after day as there was no good time to deliver that message, and I selfishly wanted as many happy days with her and the girls as possible.

Another day passed.

Walking and moving around immediately became difficult and uncomfortable for Lisa, with the growing cancer becoming physically obvious. Her liver swelled while the rest of her body was starving. A few days later, when I was pushing her around the neighborhood in a wheelchair under a brilliant blue sky, the day cool and full of fresh air, she asked, "Is this fatal?"

I continued pushing the chair. After a long pause I replied, "Yes, honey, I am afraid it is. I knew the deal, but wanted you to have a few good days with the girls and friends before we had this conversation." It was excruciating to speak the words; I felt like I had sand in my mouth. She was calm and looked up at the sky in silence.

She asked, "But why shouldn't chemotherapy improve my condition? They told me there was a chance of improvement."

I started out slowly, saying, "There is always a chance, but it is a very inexact science and it is what doctors do in our country today.

I love and trust Doctor Mac."

I stopped pushing the wheelchair on the quiet residential road and kneeled in front of her, much like I did when I asked her to marry me, and looked into her tired hazel eyes.

"Well, the problem with pancreatic cancer is that it may not be pancreatic, and doctors really do not know or understand how it acts and originates. It may be colon, bladder, liver, or others, but it shows up in multiple places and moves fast. The particularly hard thing with your case is that you have a dozen golf ball sized tumors in your liver, which is causing it to function less than 50 percent now. There is no way to slow or reverse it." I looked at her with a tear running down my cheek and both edges of my mouth about to break.

"We have a few weeks, so what will help you?" I started to push the chair again.

She thought for a long while, looking around at the trees and birds we had enjoyed in the neighborhood for years and said, "Preparing you and the girls the best we can and cleaning up this mess for your future. You have the hard job."

It was a cathartic moment. It was helpful to have a mission, definable actions with a goal in mind that we could both see ourselves progress against. So, we set out to produce three or four video messages in different locations for the girls, planned lockets for each girl with her ashes, and wrote three letters with charm bracelets specific to each of our daughters. It was a sweet and helpful process for us, the act of putting it all together. These tokens of love reminded me of a book I read in college about anticipatory grief, as my girlfriend's brother was dying of cancer. The book was full of words that made more sense now and matched with what I had just experienced. These intense emotions were anticipatory grief and the start of grief processing even before the event happened. However, the outcome of our efforts was to be a bit checkered. It was Nadir minus 21.

Our idea of the messages to the girls was that we would record a series of videos set in our favorite places, and give the girls a message from their mom to be delivered at some appropriate time in the future. We talked about what to include, what not to include, and agreed we would likely do three segments each. We would get it done in a few days, as we both knew her health was changing every minute. It would be heartfelt and inspirational for the girls to know what Mom would say about things in their future lives.

The first message was set on the beach we had enjoyed so much. After a break from the chemotherapy schedule she could walk again without help. With the melody of the ocean waves providing the background music, Lisa walked up to the camera like a newscaster doing an interview. It was a brilliant November day, about 62 degrees with a light wind blowing. Her face was slightly drawn, but only her partner of twenty-three years would be able to tell.

"Hey, it is Monday the 28th of November. We just had a big Thanksgiving with a lot of family going in and out. We are at the beach and I have a fabulous piña colada, although it is without alcohol. Can you hear me? Am I talking loud enough?" She was known to talk loud after one drink.

"This place is the best. I am so happy we are settled in and back. This is where we need to be. Girls, your great-grandma and great-grandpa started our family story, and then grandma and grandpa carried on to your Dad and I, which will continue on with your families. We found happiness, love, and a community of friends to go through life's bumpy journey. You will find this peace as well. It may take a while, but it will come. Be patient, but not too patient to grab onto the adventure."

The second message was set in the back yard of our house. We sat in our favorite teal Adirondack chairs in front of a brilliant burnt red, thirty-year-old Japanese maple, welcoming December. The sun's reflection intensified the color and made the video even more dramatic. Her face and body were changing almost daily. Her eyes were sunken, and her speech a bit slow from the morphine pump.

The pain throughout her chest and abdomen was constant.

"Hello, girls. It is now the next day, November 30. We are getting the advent calendars ready for tomorrow, and the great chocolate treats they hold for you every year. We are back from the beach and I wanted to share a few more words about how I grew up. My brothers and I lived the greatest example of what life could be because of your grandma and grandpa. They each found the love of their life and a great partner to go with them through all the ups and downs. It was a great way for us to grow up. Then the kids came along and the stresses of raising children. They were great examples of a happy life and taught me how to live well. Their example also helped me to recognize what I wanted in a husband. I hope to help you understand the same. I knew I wanted someone who was handsome, charismatic, outgoing, full of life, smart, and goal-oriented. Strong character and strength in conviction were also signatures of your dad. And most important was to find some-one who would love me more every day and not be afraid to show it. I found all of that in your dad. He is a great father. Every single day when he walks into the room, he makes me smile, laugh, and feel happier than the minute before. That tranquility is out there for you, too." She blows a kiss to the camera.

There was an unexpected interruption to our plan. Lisa had a bad reaction to an IV infusion from chemotherapy, which seemed to vary week by week, and we rushed her to the hospital. After two bags of platelets the bleeding stopped. She was yellow with jaundice. She almost died that night, and we were not finished with our messages to the girls. We had to hurry up.

This scene starts with Lisa heavily medicated, propped up in the hospital bed, barely able to keep her head from swiveling forward. It reminds me of being on an airplane, when we are unexpectedly falling asleep only to jump back into reality, startled.

"It is Tuesday, December 6th, and I just wanted to chat about Sweet Sixteen parties." She stutters with a tear in her eye. "Your grandma threw me a surprise Sweet Sixteen party, typical for a Southern girl. It was great. Charlotte, whatever you choose next year, it will be great." Her eyes well up and tears run down her cheek.

"Whether it is a big party with other girls or another trip with your dad like your tenth birthday. June, we have only three more years. And whatever you want to do will be a blast. And Rose, I cannot even imagine six more years, I cannot even imagine. I love you girls." We had to pause as she started to cry. I was out of tears and stared at her like a voyeur.

We were on a mission and losing a race against time. An hour later she continued. "So, girls: what we want to do is tell you that even though this is the hardest thing that I will ever have to do, if I fight and win I will be happy, but if I do not win, I want you to know that you are the best kids in the whole world. Even through something super horrible like this, there will be a silver lining that may not be apparent today. I will be with you in mind and spirit, every step of the way. I am a part of who you are today and tomorrow. Also, the good things that are happening in your life may not have happened if Mom was there with you physically. Everything happens for a reason. So, girls, look for the silver lining."

It was December 8. Lisa's parents came for Thanksgiving and stayed for ten days. After that, they told me they needed an emotional break as the intensity was too much. I understood. They came back immediately when she was admitted to the hospital. Still propped up in the hospital bed jaundiced, but much more alert and talkative, we continued the message. Her parents came back and walked in as we were videoing. It was a nice interaction laced with anguish of parents seeing their daughter look dramatically different than just seven days ago. Most days she was bed-ridden, but that day she managed to stand up as we pretended to dance for what turned out to be the last time. We captured small talk and then her mom filmed us dancing. We always danced to Motown, the shag a derivative of the old Lindy of the 1930s. She could not move so much, but it did not matter; I danced around her. We captured on video what the girls had seen a hundred times, us dancing. Not in the kitchen as usual, but in a hospital room. The images captured were vivid and unique as a window with shades drawn, the background with the old camera's light making the people in the picture dark. The unintended effect was brilliant as it hid the cancer. You could only see two black silhouetted images dancing against a white window. Our profile features are very clear. It will be a memorable moment for the girls.

Lisa's parents brought the girls to the hospital as we all feared any day could be the last day. We always have the camera rolling to capture fun family times, which we usually replay on Christmas Eve. So we started filming when they walked in the door. Like a hundred times before, I gave the camera to one of the girls. The oldest, Charlotte, had always wanted to be a TV weather girl. She practiced frequently on camera. June just went along with the crowd and appeared happy. Rose always wanted to tell the story, so I gave her the camera as we had done many times before. She focused on her mom and said, "This is Mommy. She has cancer, pancreas cancer."

Stone silence in the room was broken with me saying, "Yes, we know." She continued going around the room introducing everyone. For some reason, she had drawn a red arrow on the top of her left hand pointing to her middle knuckle. Holding the camera with her right hand, she shot the camera down her hand and pointed using the arrow on her hand to explain who each person was and what they were doing. It was hilarious, and a well-needed reprieve from the emotional exhaustion.

She flipped the camera around, smiled, and said, "I am pausing filming now." It was probably the last time I saw that little girl.

CHAPTER XI

Creating Future Memories

AS A WELCOME RELIEF, Lisa was discharged from the hospital on December 8. We were frantically trying to tie up loose ends and grasp at our final moments together. We thought an interestingly crafted heart locket on a necklace chain containing some of their mother's ashes would be a nice gift for the girls, a positive reminder that Mom was always with them. We also wrote three different letters—from Mom to her daughters—with a charm bracelet for each girl, a popular gift at the time for daughters.

The actual letters are on reproduced on the next few pages, with the charm bracelet choices discussed in detail. The individual letters started out the same, then became specific for each girl.

December 8, 2005

Dearest Daughter:

I hope you enjoy this charm bracelet as much as I enjoyed putting it together for you. This little project made me think of the many, many special times we've shared together—both just you and me, and as a family.

What makes a charm special is that it represents memories of fun times, great laughs, trips taken, and lessons learned. What makes a bracelet special is that it is made of links, so you can think of it as one of the many links you'll always have to me.

I thought you'd enjoy having these charms now, and I've put a few away for later, too.

Mom's Bracelet for the Charming Charlotte

Tarheel Charm

No matter where you live, you'll always have some tar on your heels. I know you'll have your pick of colleges if you work hard!

My Locket Charm

You look like both Dad and me, but you definitely have my smile… not to mention my personality! I've always felt like I could guess what and how you feel, just because our karma is so alike. I love you.

Annapolis Charm

Dad and I will always be happy we made the move to Annapolis for many reasons. We had a lot of fun times and made new friends, but the move also brought our family—and particularly, you and your sisters—much closer together. You three had to rely on each other much more than ever before. Remember the great times in Annapolis when you see this charm, and also let it remind you that you will always be able to rely on your sisters.

Washington, DC Charm

One great thing about our move to Annapolis was being close to DC. You'll always know more about our nation's capital than many of your friends, and have great memories of Eastern Market, the zoo, museums, July 4th fireworks over the Washington Monument, riding in the limo to the Jefferson Memorial in the moonlight, *A Christmas Carol* at Ford's Theater, and *The Nutcracker* with all of us and Mimi and Papa too.

ooooo

Sombrero Charm

This is to remind you of the favorite foods that we share—Mexican, sushi, edamame, and fondue. Let it remind you to always keep some spice in your life!

Megaphone Charm

You'll always be "head" cheerleader in my book. With our smile, enthusiasm, and great cheer—you'll go far!

Book Charm

To Kill a Mockingbird has always been my favorite book. When you read it (or reread it), I think you'll know why. Enjoy!

Cell Phone Charm

Just had to get this charm, even though we gave the cell phone to you as kind of a bribe! However, cell phones are a wonderful tool to keep your friendships strong. I believe we can never have too many strong, close friendships in life. It's easy to think that you will always have good friends, just like I've always had. It takes a great friend to be one.

T-Shirt Charm

You have great style and grace, and an uncanny ability to put clothes together. You already have such panache—you're destined to be a trendsetter and style maker!

Mom's Bracelet for the Charming June

Tennis Racquet Charm

I am so happy you are enjoying tennis and becoming such a good player. It is one of the many things about you that are so much like me! If you keep it up, there's no telling how far you can go, but the most important thing is to have fun!

Annapolis Charm

Dad and I will always be happy we made the move to Annapolis for many reasons. We had a lot of fun times and made new friends, but the move also brought our family—and particularly, you and your sisters—much closer together. You three had to rely on each other much more than ever before. Remember the great times in Annapolis when you see this charm, and also let it remind you that you will always be able to rely on your sisters.

Statue of Liberty Charm

You know New York is my favorite city, and I hope this charm always reminds you of all the exciting times we had together in the city. I am just so glad you love New York almost as much as I do! And remember, you can always be a "city" girl wherever you live by being open to new experiences, enjoying different people, loving exotic foods, and on and on—just like you already do!

My Locket Charm

Everyone said you looked just like me when you were a baby, and I was so proud. Now you look like both Dad and me! You'll always be my super star! I love you.

TV Charm

We've had so many fun times... traveling to cool cities, playing on the beach, eating out at fun restaurants, swimming in our pools and hot tubs, jumping on the trampoline... the list could go on and on. But sometimes just sitting around with you, Charlotte, and Rose watching silly TV shows is the best. Remember, it's not always what you do that's most important, but who you do it with. Keep riding your Holy Grail coconut horse!

Tarheel Charm

No matter where you live, you'll always have some tar on your heels. I know you'll have your pick of colleges if you work hard!

Bell Charm

I bet you were puzzled by the church bell? Fooled you…it is a "Taco Bell!"

Puppy Dog Charm

I had to get this cute dog because I know you love animals so much. Your loving and caring nature will only grow more beautiful as you grow older.

Special Sister Charm

You know how much I cherish my relationships with Jeffie and Ronnie. My brothers are my most favorite people in the world, but sisters can be something very special too. I know it can be hard being the middle sister, June, but I hope you will always appreciate that you have Charlotte and Rose. They're your special sisters and you are theirs. Always love, respect, and enjoy each other.

Mom's Bracelet for the Charming Rose

Cute as a Button Charm

Guess I do not have to explain why I chose this charm, do I? You'll always be cute as a button, but remember "pretty is as pretty does." Love you!

Flip Flops Charm

Remember all the fun times we had at the beach? Topsail, Wrightsville, St. Augustine, the Florida Keys? You'll probably always have sand in your shoes and want to live near the beach—just like Dad and me.

Mom & Babe Charm

Always remember that the day you were born was one of the happiest days of my life. I figure you can guess the other three dates (don't forget Dad's and my wedding day). You were the cutest baby! Still can't decide if you look more like me or more like Mimi! Your smile and sparkle will inspire so many people!

Washington, DC Charm

On great thing about our move to Annapolis was being close to DC. You'll always know more about our nation's capital than many of your friends, and have great memories of Eastern Market, the zoo, museums, July 4th fireworks over the Washington Monument, riding in the limo to the Jefferson Memorial in the moonlight, *A Christmas Carol* at Ford's Theater, and *The Nutcracker* with all of us and Mimi and Papa too.

Tarheel Charm

No matter where you live, you'll always have some tar on your heels. I know you'll have your pick of colleges if you work hard!

Annapolis Charm

Dad and I will always be happy we made the move to Annapolis for many reasons. We had a lot of fun times and made new friends, but the move also brought our family—and particularly, you and your sisters—much closer together. You three had to rely on each other much more than ever before. Remember the great times in Annapolis when you see this charm, and also let it remind you that you will always be able to rely on your sisters.

Mom's Locket Charm

A lot of people tell me that you look like me and I find that such a compliment! It makes me happy that you act a little like me too, but you are a unique, bright shining star—wide open and not afraid to try anything!

Rose, you may wear this as often or as little as you like, knowing that my heart and spirit are always with you. This bracelet is merely a symbol of the boundless love I have for you.

Your Mom Forever,

xoxoxo Mom

These letters to her nine-, twelve-, and fifteen-year-old daughters were heartfelt, and helped Lisa ease her pain of leaving daughters motherless in the world. If that was her only goal, it was a success.

Looking forward to the reality of giving them what we thought would be an endearing gesture proved to be a different mindset. Teenage girls are interested in what teenage girls are interested in, which is somewhat variable and unpredictable. Their reaction was varied from "What is this?" to "Mom's ashes?" to "Wear it?" to "Do I have to?"

With a pang of anguish, I said, "No, but keep it for a keepsake in the future."

Conceiving of the lockets, charm bracelets, and videos was helpful for Lisa as she transitioned out of this life, leaving her daughters alone to navigate the future without a mother. We both thought the ideas were great and had no regrets. We were both wrong. Retrospectively, a decade later, I think waiting a few years may have been helpful in giving the girls a more panoramic emotional viewpoint of the letters and lockets. However, I did give them each a CD of family pictures, Christmas videos, and a video message from their mom after five years, and the response was the same. What I can say is that I feel good about them having these things, and that is enough.

At the time it seemed to create more anxiety about loss, almost like a shackle for the future. The gifts were not freeing, uplifting, or comforting to the girls, rather a depressing long-term symbol for their loss. Linda, one of Lisa's best friends, grabbed me on the side at home one day during the last two weeks of Lisa's life, and told me about how she grew up as an adopted child and never heard her mother's voice. She made a good point, so I set out to make recordings for the girls, so they could hear their mother's voice whenever they wanted to. Five years later, I gave the girls digitized photos and videos of their mom talking, just so they would have a record. Only Rose had an interest in seeing the video, and still gains a "second wind" from watching it. If they looked at the pictures and videos, they did not tell me. I can only guess why.

They may want to remember her as she was in their young minds. It is not a surprise that they do not generally talk about their mom or mention the video. It may be okay, and they have completely processed that part of their grief. Unprocessed emotions have the staying power to saddle your present life and relationships with undue past baggage, risking inconsistent and inappropriate responses to current situations. This perspective is confusing to your friends, family, and relationships.

For each step of the way, it has been helpful for me to focus on the emotions or feelings of grief, anxiety, or related thoughts at the earliest possible moment that I can recognize and identify. If I then isolate the thought and attach a label to it (e.g. great family memory surfing), giving it a size, shape, and color (e.g. big bright sun on deep blue ocean water with dried salt on my face from swimming), it seems to help me process the emotion better, and incorporate it into my grieving process rather than upsetting the apple cart as a grief trigger. That is, you can either think of that happy memory of swimming together at the beach, or a sad thought about something that has been lost. I choose to relive the joy from that moment. Listen to your own thoughts. You can either process them when you first feel them, or put them in the appropriate context for later consideration.

CHAPTER XII

Nadir: The Lowest Point in the Fortunes of a Person

OF COURSE, IT WAS MORE INTENSE seeing it play out in front of my eyes. All five senses were continually in hyperdrive for those last forty-two days. In many ways, it was as if I was more alert and alive than ever before. I could see, hear, and take in 100 percent of what was transpiring in my world. It was excruciatingly painful and awe-inspiring in the same instant.

I knew the end was close by the description hospice workers had provided. Her breathing pattern was noticeably different. It started to resemble the Lamaze pattern of three short and one long breath: phew, phew, phew and pheeewww, pause. I remembered it well as her delivery coach for the three girls. Ironically, the breathing process was intended to help manage pain as you bring life into the world. It worked three times, and I was thankful as it made me feel calm and transition was near. It went on for several hours as I talked to her like a senator on the filibuster trail. I remembered a passage from Emerson's "Self-Reliance" that I wanted to read and ran to get the book. Just as I found the book and started down the steps, I heard her call my name. She had not spoken in two days or eaten in ten. It could have been my imagination or fatigue or hallucination, but it seemed quite normal at the time. Maybe it was a last energy burst that allowed her to speak my name. A tearful smile came over me as I watched her slip away.

I knew she was in transition and her passing was close. I read the chapter from one of my all-time favorite books that she also liked, as it personified our journey together. Emerson's passage on self-reliance had always spoken deeply to me, as conformity is not in my DNA:

"The voyage of the best ship is a zigzag line of a hundred tacks. See the line from a sufficient distance, and it straightens itself to the average tendency. Your genuine action will explain itself and will explain your other genuine actions. Your conformity explains nothing. Act singly, and what you have already done singly will justify you now."

—*Ralph Waldo Emerson, "Self-Reliance"*

This passage seemed to capture a course chart of our twenty-three-year marriage, our children's paths, our professional lives, business paths, and relationships. At that moment, reading that passage to Lisa at her intersection seemed to sum up everything. In our own unique way, we traveled a sea of a hundred tacks in our time together, and from a distance, it formed a trend—happy, successful, caring, engaged, and present—a beautiful life.

Her breathing became more rhythmic with short, shallow breaths, and she struggled to keep her eyes open. This went on for a time as I told her she was free to go when she needed to. "Why are you hanging on so hard? Are you trying to get to the 17th?" We were four months short of our 24th wedding anniversary on April 17. Her breathing paused, and her facial expression changed, which I interpreted as a yes with a smile. Her eyes opened as her breathing turned to a slower, deeper rhythm. This pattern drifted to seconds between breaths.

And then she took one last breath and stopped.

Her eyes were open. I tried to close them with two fingers like in the movies, but it did not work. I tried again, same result. In a moment of panic, I found myself praying. *Please, God, let her eyes close.* I tried one more time, and it worked.

I snipped the bud of a white rose someone had given to us, and put it on her pillow beside her face. After waking her parents, the four of us spent some time alone before calling hospice. It was the first peaceful moment we had known in forty-two days. The 1,008 hours felt like years.

The latest statistics suggest only 12 percent of all marriages are happy. What a shame. Losing a spouse in the prime of life after twenty-three years, three brilliant girls, and thousands of great memories is a devastating, life-changing event. Because my wife and I had no regrets and lived most days to the fullest, the transition had been easier as it had not been plagued with regret, remorse, or replays. I kept thinking that there must be a silver lining to this terrible situation. For the longest time, the silver lining was not so clear.

Before the end of this story, it will be.

The excruciating minutes, hours, days, and months that followed the first days of her passing were numbing. Getting out of bed the first few days was hard. It was made a bit easier by having three wounded teenage girls, because you think of them more than yourself. But it was difficult. A friend gave me a book about bad things happening to good people. It did not help. Time moved on, but life as I knew it was in a new unrecognizable, dissociative state. My face felt like a glass windowpane, about to break into a thousand shards. Can you hear the glass shearing one molecule at a time? It is your soul trying to stay together. *Just hang on one more day,* I kept telling myself. *You have three young daughters to help through this, just hang on . . . one more day. If not for yourself, then for them.*

It is important in the healing process to not put your deceased spouse on a pedestal beyond reproach. Your friends and relatives will likely do that, and sometimes unintentionally at the expense of your feelings, emotions, and thoughts. For the most part it is not intentional or malicious, just human nature coping with a great loss. But it still hurts and does not always make sense. There is no need to rewrite history, it was great already! But that is what happens. Some will be stricken with revisionist history of their new perceptions of things that transpired. That is, some perceptions of events and the roles people played in our lives and what was going on suddenly becomes skewed.

We are all human, we all grieve differently. No one likes everything anyone does all the time. Be honest with yourself and friends. The latter will be more difficult, because they did not know the daily interactions between you and your spouse and will take the slightest comment as an insult to their friend, your partner. They will be obliged to readily share this with you. Tread lightly, but be aware it impacts how you feel about yourself, and your future. Not even the most well-intentioned spouse is perfect, and it is helpful to reward yourself with the truth. I did this, and she did or did not do this or that. Not nitpicking, but reaffirming your contribution and theirs. We were a team, and we worked well together.

As the surviving spouse, do not sell your contribution short, for others may. Again, it is not intentional or mean, it is just surprising that the reverence for the deceased outshines the needs of the grieving present. Some friends will fall victim to this emotional virus. The good news is that a great number of your friends are immune to it.

CHAPTER XIII

Can You Ask Your Mom if I Can Spend the Night This Weekend?

ALDERMAN ELEMENTARY SCHOOL IS a fabulous neighborhood school built in the 1970s, complete with concrete floors and *That '70s Show* aesthetic at every turn.

The school is a bustling community of almost 600 students, first through sixth grade. For some reason, it was a personal badge of success for me to drop the kids off at school every morning. While only a five-minute drive from our house, we always had fun discussions, and I loved the routine of making the girls breakfast beforehand. They may not remember, but I do. "Take a risk today, I'm proud of you," was the last thing I'd say to them before dropping them off at school.

It was just another coastal North Carolina day in mid-March: mid-60s, a gentle breeze kissing your face, and a crystal-clear sky. Calm, relaxing, and bordering on spiritual. Neither Rose nor I was prepared for what was about to happen next.

As the girls returned from recess and sat at their desks, a friend asked Rose, "Can you ask your mom if we can come over to your house after school this Friday?"

Rose's face froze. She did not move, breathe, or blink. Her mouth hung open; her eyes were fixed. She had no mom to ask if her friends could come over. The classroom she knew and loved so well spontaneously shrank to the size of a thimble with the air exiting like a tornado. Her body was rigid, her face beet-red. She burst into tears and her friends did not understand at first. By the time they did, she had wet her pants and was totally humiliated. What could be worse for a nine-year-old halfway through fourth grade?

Fortunately, her teacher Ms. Newton put it all together pretty fast and took her to the nurse.

"Do you want me to call your dad, sweetie?" Ms. Newton asked. No reply, just more convulsive crying.

"I think I should," Ms. Newton said. "Okay?"

The principal called me and let me know what was going on.

"Can you pick her up?"

"Yes, of course," I said.

Once there, I tried to get Rose into a better headspace.

"Hey, let's go to lunch," I said to her.

"Not hungry," she said. Silence prevailed as we drove. On impulse, I made a turn in the opposite direction of home. At first, she did not notice. After a while, she caught on.

"What's up? Where are we going? Not to see Kathleen, I hope?" Kathleen was our neighborhood friend, and a therapist I engaged with to give us all guidance in grieving.

"No, not Kathleen. I need to run to the grocery store," I said.

"Oh. Okay."

I had an idea. It was risky, but it was worth a shot.

The grocery store had always been a good diversion for the girls, as each girl got to choose something that a parent approved of. They also had to listen to Dad drone on about label design, product positioning, and why certain things were in certain places, as I had worked in the retail business before.

Today, she chose Mentos gum. It was a good choice, as chewing gum always relieves tension, reduces stress, and helps serve as a distraction. As we made it through the grocery store's 100,000 items, we came to the produce section. It was stuffed with freshly cut daffodils in stainless metal peck size buckets. Throughout the past twenty years, there is hardly a day where our house does not have fresh-cut flowers of some sort.

"Hey, Rose, the daffodils came in this week. How about we get some for your mom?" I said.

"Mom? What? Where?" she said. She looked completely confused. She paused, doing her best to regain her thoughts.

"Where would we take them?"

"How about the church garden, where some of her ashes are? Her name is carved in marble on the wall there, too. Or how about the beach, since we put most of her ashes in the ocean?"

"Yeah," she said, "that would be great."

We bought a big bunch of freshly cut daffodils for $4.99 and headed downtown to the church. No one was there when we arrived. We placed the daffodils in the church garden where we buried some of her mom's ashes only three months earlier. It was peaceful as we said a prayer, and then we talked to her mom.

"We love you and miss you, sweet mother," Rose said.

We took another bouquet to the other side of the garden, to the marble wall with the list of dearly departed church members. Slowly and with care, we rubbed our fingers over every letter of Lisa's name in the white etched marble wall. Methodically tracing each letter was mesmerizing and comforting for us both. With only three months after her death, it still didn't feel real or even possible that my wife of twenty-three years was gone.

There was a peaceful silence in the car as we headed toward the ocean. Looking out the window, Rose finally broke the silence.

"Dad, what do I say when someone asks me to ask my mom if they can come over?"

"Tell them you'll ask me instead," I said.

She smiled. "Of course, Dad."

We drove the rest of the fifteen-minute drive to the beach in silence, yet a rare serenity laid between us. As we arrived at the ocean, I recalled that cold day in January where we first put her ashes in the sea.

CHAPTER XIV

Charlotte Ten Years Later: Nadir Plus 3,650 Days

I AM NOW TWENTY-FIVE YEARS OLD, living in Denver and working for a marketing company. High school, dating, college, first job, and a great new apartment are all in my rearview mirror. But haunting my rearview mirror and my windshield straight ahead is that little pang of remorse. I still miss Mom, not only on the days that are obvious (such as birthdays, graduations, and significant life events), but in the mundane path of daily life when I am having a bad day and just want to call my mom. A security blanket, a kind word, a reassuring tone—*It will be okay, honey*—is all I need to hear. Dad tries his best, but a mother's touch is a mother's touch.

Dad went to the 100th birthday party of a relative recently and shared how what he saw made him think a lot about his three daughters. He described how the pictures through the life span of one hundred years was a fascinating chronology of history. The telephones, radio, television, the differences in clothing, furniture, cars, airplanes, and just about everything around her life had changed. Then he said something that really stuck with me: "In her 100 years she has seen ten decades of change. Think about how much has changed in our lives in the last decade and multiply that by ten. That is the amount of change we have to look forward to in our lifetime." That thought was oddly comforting to me. I am not sure how I will carry these emotions about losing my mom going forward, whether they will grow or shrink as I peel back life's adventure. I do know that I will miss her on my engagement day, rehearsal dinner, wedding day, announcing a child (maybe), moving in to my first home, asking for decorating tips, and a slew of other potential future moments. My stepmom fills that great void in all of those times, and I am thankful I have her.

When I was fifteen, I was so self-absorbed that the grief honestly did not hit me that hard. I didn't really deal with it for years. It wasn't until I started college that stuff started bubbling up. I joined a grief group my freshman year. It was tremendously helpful to find women with similar experiences and feelings. One of my roommates in college lost her mom too, so it was easy to share our emotions with each other, and because of our bond, we're still friends today. Still, The Parent Died Club isn't exactly the best place to meet someone.

At some point you are just too exhausted to be angry. It is like that psychological concept of learned helplessness, with the dog in the cage that is randomly shocked with electricity. You know the shocks are coming, so you just lie down and take it because there is no other way. I still get anxious and scared when I am too happy, because I'm waiting for something bad to happen. I need to work on reducing that fear.

I get through all of the down moments knowing that I choose to be happy and live a full life, but you do not forget.

CHAPTER XV

June Ten Years Later: Nadir Plus 3,650 Days

I AM NOW TWENTY-TWO YEARS OLD. College was fun, but a struggle. I fell into the usual college student potholes. Bad guy boyfriend, partying too much, sorority fun, and not quite knowing what I wanted to do in life.

I've been on a bit of an emotional rollercoaster for the vast majority of college, in part due to my mom's death when I was twelve. I just couldn't get on an even keel. I felt a bit empty and was always looking for something around the corner. While I have a tendency to speak my mind, I still end up hiding my true emotions. I think it's mainly due to losing my mom at such a young age. I couldn't find any meaning or direction in my life after she passed away. I understood she was sick and died but living with her death impacted me more than I realized at the time. I kept it deep inside, and still get emotional when talking to people about my mom.

I learned how rocky the ride could be even later. It seems that everyone gets sad and thinks about death at different times. I did too. You never know what will trigger memories of your parents or mom, but it will be sudden. For me, it was a backpack she bought me when I was eleven years old. I still had it in my closet, but didn't use it. I went into the student bookstore at college and there it was, almost the same backpack for sale. I just stared at it for a few minutes, remembering the joy of the gift then and the memory of the loss. I couldn't help it, I started crying. It was a quiet cry that I did not share with anyone. It felt like a transition from sadness and mourning for Mom to celebrating her. She went to college and had done the same things I was doing, and now she was there with me.

The funniest situations can trigger memories, good and bad.

CHAPTER XVI

Rose Ten Years Later: Nadir Plus 3,650 Days

IN THE YEARS BETWEEN fifth and seventh grade I had lost my mom, moved, lost friends, and changed schools three times in two years. I decided that I just didn't want to lose any more. I preferred to be alone.

I stopped reaching out to people and started turning inward. I spent more time pretending to shop for clothes online. I refused to talk about my emotions with therapists all along the way. I wouldn't talk much with my dad. I couldn't share my true feelings with anyone. I kept it all pent up. I don't know why, it's just what I did. I did not want to run with the popular girls, or the pretty girls. I don't think I'm pretty, and it's hard for me to believe that people really like me. I didn't experiment much with drugs during high school, only occasionally. My family saw my anxiety and depression mostly rearing its head between November 4 (Mom's diagnosis date) and December 16 (Mom's death date) every year. I went to a psychiatrist, but never revealed the truth. I had stockpiled the antidepressants, Adderall, and other drugs, preferring not to take them.

As the youngest of three, it wasn't hard to get away with always being too young to wash the dishes and feign ignorance of chores. It really was a part of a bigger desire to just hide and not participate. I turned eighteen years old and went off to the college of my choice. I had four years of fully funded freedom ahead of me. I went to a university as a freshman and had a pretty rough semester. I didn't care about grades, going to class, sorority functions, or anything. I have struggled with depression for about ten years now; it started right after my mom passed away. Dad was not Mom, my sisters were teenage girls and acting like it, and I felt all alone. When my depression started getting louder and speaking over my internal voice, I started to get self-destructive. All I wanted to do was get out of my own head, and drugs and alcohol did that for me. They made me feel numb, which was the only way I could get through my daily life. I didn't ease into my escape plan, I jumped off the deep end.

Home from my first semester of college was supposed to be a relief, a celebration and a restful period of time. It was not. I spent the last three months avoiding everything. Avoiding things got me through high school; surely it would work again. I avoided chances to make new friends, have coffee with sorority sisters, engage in classes, and meet classmates. Most of all, I avoided responsibility and accountability. It was just what I had done for the last ten years—hide from life. I embraced drugs because it helped me avoid reality. It set me free. Little did I know it was putting me in an emotional prison. Cocaine, Xanax, marijuana, heroin, meth and lots of alcohol: what's not to like? Xanax is the drug that made me totally uninhibited. It was like my filter for fear and good judgment just went away. Xanax also eliminated the idea of a consequence for my actions and totally eliminated my moral gyroscope.

No one else knew my secret, until I decided to go visit Mommy.

I was really good at hiding my true feelings and emotions. I did not want anyone to know how I was really feeling, so I put on a good face and acted happy all the time. After a while it got easier, like pretending to be happy and energetic at school when I had just cried in the bathroom a minute ago. Talking about my feelings is probably the most uncomfortable thing for me, right next to crying in front of people, so keeping all of my emotions to myself was not hard.

The first time I thought about killing myself was when I was twelve years old in sixth grade. I did not see the point in living anymore because every day was a struggle. Everything seemed bleak; I was just going through the motions of life and not enjoying it. The thought of suicide was always with me, like a jacket in the closet, and whenever something in life got hard, I would always turn to that as an option. In sixth grade, I started self-destructive behavior, mostly cutting myself where no one could see, and as the years went on, it just got worse. The year I turned sixteen was when my bulimia started, because it made me feel in control. I don't know why.

In college, the drugs only made my depression worse. I felt okay when I was loaded, but the second I started coming down was very dangerous territory. I only felt happy and good about myself when I was high, so why not be high all the time?

After failing most of my classes that first semester, I came home hoping I could see my old friends and just relax. But since my dealer left early for winter break, I came home with no cocaine and a bad attitude. I only remember the first day I got home, everything else is a blur. One minute I was drinking, snorting bars of Xanax and having a good time, and the next thing I knew, I was waking up in the hospital, asking my dad what happened. Dad said when he found me, I was in my room passed out in a pile of my own puke with empty pill bottles all around me and a suicide note. I didn't remember anything.

Ten years later I am living in California. To be honest, I was hesitant about writing this. I wasn't sure if I wanted my personal struggles and what I went through to be public, but after thinking about it for a while, I decided it shouldn't be something that I keep hidden. I'm really anxious about people knowing what happened, but I am not embarrassed about it. People can think what they want, but I am proud of who I am and that is all that matters.

I struggle with addiction and have visited 27 programs over the years, ranging from one week to a three month stay. I mean it every time when I say that I want to stay sober, but more times than not, it's hard to follow through.

I am sad, ashamed, and feel guilty for what I have done to my family.

CHAPTER XVII

Mothers and Daughters

CAN THERE BE A MORE DISORIENTING, breathtaking, everlasting event in a girl's life than the loss of her mother?

It seems that part of the answer may lie in the Optimist Creed, "Keep your eye upon the doughnut, not upon the hole." It holds great wisdom for us all. But as human beings it seems it is far too easy for us to focus on what's missing in our doughnut, or to focus on everyone else's doughnut. In processing grief, it is crucial to focus on what you have and what your new life looks like. Daily positive affirmations, smiley notes around the house, and any other positive reminders to break through negative thoughts are extremely valuable, and will help bridge the vulnerable periods.

I fought off the sadness when talking to my daughters every day, for what they were going to miss out on without their mom there to turn to and talk with. Dads are important in many of the same respects, but a mom fills a particular part of a young girl's role when growing up as a woman. From the big birthdays of ten, sixteen, eighteen and twenty-one, to making the cheerleading squad, cheering at every football game, making the tennis team, high school graduation, deciding on which colleges to apply to, choosing the right college, sorority rush, selection of major, parents weekend every year, college graduation day, first job interview, first job acceptance, serious dating, engagement, marriage, first apartment, first home, pregnant, first born, christening, second born, first day of preschool, first day of school, first day of middle school, first day of high school, high school graduation... and it goes on and on and on and will always be with you. Oh yes, and there is a special day every year to remind you of your loss... Mother's Day, thanks Hallmark. It is the silent elephant in the room, unless you out it.

Mother's Day, Nadir plus 152 days. It was just like many other Sundays: breakfast before going to church, landing in the pew one minute before the 9:00 a.m. service starts (an Episcopalian tradition). I noticed the church calendar at breakfast said *Mother's Day Service*, but I did not say anything to the girls, as it had only been five months since their mother passed away. The Sunday service was a traditional Episcopalian routine: up and down a lot, six stanzas to every song, and 250 parishioners, many of which I only see at church.

Then the minister said, "Will all children and teens come up to the altar? We have a flower for you to give to your mother for Mother's Day, a white rose."

I could barely breathe. The girls were all miraculously not at home the night she died; they did not see their mom dead, or the white rose I put next to her, but did they know about it? Had their grandparents, Lisa's parents, told them?

All three girls slowly looked at me, tears welling up in their eyes.

"Dad, don't make us go up there," they said.

I was a fairly strict dad and made them do things many times that they did not want to do. This time, however, I reached out and took their hands in mine. Thinking the worst of it had passed, none of us were prepared for the children of the church bouncing back to their seats, proudly presenting a white rose to their mothers. Lots of hugging, kissing, and laughter ensued. Everyone seemed happy. I didn't notice that there was an empty seat next to me until a well-meaning friend brought his rose over and put it next to us on the empty chair. I smiled at the girls to dissuade their reaction, but I was screaming inside, my friend's gesture having added to the emotional pressure all four of us were already feeling. We were learning how to deal with the unexpected reminders, the intrusions into an otherwise happy day—grief triggers.

Of course it's okay to cry, but sometimes you're just so exhausted from it, especially when you're grieving over the loss of a loved one. You just want to feel normal, like the rest of the world in your environment.

It was the last Mother's Day that the girls and I went to church.

On some Mother's Day in the future, I hope the girls will be able to celebrate their mom with joy and happiness and only a small sting of loss. Loss is a powerful emotion, worthy of leading, driving, and empowering a positive contribution to your life, or it is draining and depleting, leading to a dismal free fall into obscurity. How can you maintain the focus on the beauty in life scarred by such a loss? How do you look forward through the windshield of life rather than focusing on the rearview mirror of what happened yesterday?

I also worry that if they have not worked through their mother's early death that my eventual passing may elicit a double whammy response. That is, if they keep processing their mother's grief individually, everything will be okay because at Dad's passing, they will be grieving mostly for their dad. But if they do not embrace a continued grieving for their mom, it may be a bigger event.

Since their mom's passing, I hear the tension in their voices if I get the slightest cold, along with a plethora of questions concerning how I'm feeling. My youngest frequently says that she does not want to call me sometimes because she knows I worry about her, and she fears it puts too much stress on me. I just want each of my three sweet daughters to focus on what they have and can have—A Beautiful Life.

CHAPTER XVIII

Grief Triggers in Everyday Life

SOME PEOPLE DO NOT LIKE THE CONCEPT of grief triggers as it gives up responsibility for your actions. Grief triggers are intensely emotional feelings that remind you of the person, the magnitude of the loss, or the continuum of all emotional feelings with which one must deal. Either way, these thoughts are acute onset, intense, visceral emotions to which you will react in an unprepared fashion as they ambush you in an instant.

A funeral is not a grief trigger. Throughout antiquity, funerals are social events that honor the deceased, but are mostly to support the living by showing respect and acknowledging change.

The ability to understand and embrace changes in our environment through our five senses is part of makes us uniquely human. Throughout our lives, we develop associations with each of the senses that brings us great pleasure and happiness. When turned upside down, all of the five senses trigger vivid thoughts, remembrances, and emotional upheavals in an instant and at any given time. These intensely personal packets of emotions, grief triggers, landmines, eggshells, grenades—or however you decide to label them—are very real and very powerful. It is important to acknowledge them.

Do not sweep them under the carpet or they will accumulate, and you will not be able to clean them up or process them further.

A key to successfully processing grief is learning to build coping mechanisms for grief triggers. These unexpected intersections of normal present life and intensely emotional past experiences are highly charged. The experience can be paralyzing, sickening, gut wrenching, numbing, saddening, but also stimulating, rewarding and remarkable at the same time. If you can get to a point that the trigger is a way to celebrate what you had rather than what you lost, the trigger becomes a rewarding positive moment. Seeing a photo, or a piece of art you purchased as a couple, a shirt, a towel, a tennis bag, a car, a brush, glasses, a cocktail napkin, a margarita glass, a pan, a food smell, the touch of a special material, the sound of wine glasses clinking, and little things you would never have suspected to cause such grief, will remind you of the range of experiences with your spouse. Almost everyone has experienced loss of some sort and the grief triggers that follow. These triggers can be converted from a sad moment into fond memories of a robust love and, in some ways, the converted trigger preserves the memory, rather than demeaning or distorting it.

Grief triggers can also be tied to your daily routine. As a very active parent of three girls, I always helped with homework, cooked, cleaned, disciplined, went to as many school lunches, plays, and functions as possible. I shopped for them frequently. After my wife died, I continued these routines, but I was not prepared for just how very different my peer group viewed my situation, the family, my role, and my experiences.

One unusual grief trigger was that my friends put my wife on a pedestal with no blemishes in order to deal with her passing. I could not understand that, as I knew her best; for better or worse, we all have our flaws. My contribution to the relationship and even our family seemed to instantly vanish from everyone's mind, that I did all the cooking and cleaning and earned all the money, or that I didn't play golf on the weekends because it cut into my time with the girls. Everyone suddenly thought, *How will the girls survive?* It was as if I hadn't been totally loyal for twenty-four years and in the parenting trenches every day for the last 15 years. And this was the experience that replayed over and over and over again. A portion of my peer group was so uncomfortable, they almost acted as if I was a stranger. I was not prepared for this unusual treatment from people I knew. I did not expect it. After all, they were my friends too, right?

I was not prepared for the discomfort and isolation my peers inadvertently saddled me with because they were grief-stricken. I was not prepared for their grief triggers. Everyone deals with adversity in his or her own way based on the sum of genetics, cumulative experiences, and current living environments.

Early in the grieving process, I was confused, numb, and oblivious to the walking coma I called my life. On one such day, it was 45 degrees and rainy. I always put together an interesting breakfast to stimulate the brilliance and emerging genius of my fifth, eighth, and eleventh grade children. This day was no different. Cheese grits, bacon, and toast; what better smell can there be than bacon and toast in the air? My girls and I play a game to come up with new concoctions of taste sensations, while trying to avoid the obvious and absurd. That day I knew I had a winner: a bacon and cheese grits sandwich. When I was young, my dad always got up early and cooked breakfast for my brother, sister, mother, and me. He drew on his short order cook days in college and Army experience, introducing delicacies such as SOS (look it up in the Army Field Manual), beef tips, and the like. From my perspective, I wasn't breaking any new ground, just emulating my parental model. But today I knew I had a winner. I turned the music up louder than usual (we always played music in the morning; like coffee it gets you going, and that day it was one of the girls' favorites, "Mamma Mia").

Sometimes your mind follows the math of musical rhythm and is soothing to the soul.

"Okay, girls. My entry is a grits sandwich. First, cut a piece of toast in half. Apply a healthy slather of cheese grits to one half, top with too much bacon, and feast."

"Oh yeah," my eleven-year-old said, taking the other half of toast. "You take a piece of toast, apply a thin layer of butter, followed by a thin layer of concord grape jelly, top it with bacon, and spatter it with cheese grits." Victory as the message of life's little pleasures was passed along to the next generation.

After dropping my youngest off at school, I was off to Sam's Club for household staples and grocery shopping before 10:00 a.m. (only business owners are allowed in that early, while consumers have to wait at the door). I stocked up on the usual and proceeded to get lost in the twilight zone that is Sam's Club. It was a normal day in my new life. Until, that is, I saw Dana. Dana was a walking buddy of my wife and an acquaintance of mine. Lisa was her informal therapist, as Dana tended to dump her emotional bucket frequently. Dana was prone to talk, on the phone and in person. Unfortunately, it's easier for some people to focus on the negative, discount the good, and negate the normal life challenges of others. My wife struggled with some of the things Dana would say, but was passionate about trying to open up her way of thinking.

My cart was about full when I first saw her. Dana's a tall, attractive blonde with pretty eyes and a sad face. She always struggled with a cordial hello, but I could tell she was trying. As our eyes met, I sought to find the solace in a friend of almost a decade.

She took one look at me with my groceries and flowers and started crying. She remembered that we always had flowers in our house and commented just the week before that I seemed to abandon the fun practice. She was right. For some reason I did not buy flowers for a couple of months. Maybe my unconscious mind was grieving too. We hugged and had a short conversation about schools and kids. She profusely apologized about crying as she continued to cry. We are all unique, yet most of us can be grouped into categories according to our culture, habits, or experiences. How we deal with sudden trauma or grief is no different. Dana seemed to be in the slow to no grief process, just not acknowledging that today's situation was actually true.

I happened into another grief trigger later in the afternoon—a sweet-smelling alcohol cleanser sent my thoughts to the doctor's office, specifically to the time when Lisa was first diagnosed. It was years ago that Jack diagnosed my wife, but that day I was reliving that moment in his office because of some random grief trigger. It is hard to believe that I am reliving a painful year all because of a smell. Smells and sounds are reminiscent and associated strongly with memory. You walk into the bright, fluorescent lit entrance, and in any other situation would think, *What a nice office.* The beautiful olive-green walls were accented with oil paintings of interesting, calming scenes. A painting with a small sailboat hung crooked on the wall, along with a series of oil paintings that looked like depictions of Jackson Hole, Wyoming. The trees were taller on the East Coast, and mountains smiled in the background.

The usual sounds of names being called out broke the silence of the typical physician's waiting room. Mrs. Jones, Mr. Jackson, family of Brooks, the Stevens's family. Adrenaline rushes through your veins when your name is called in any situation, but in this environment, it is like being called to the principal or getting pulled over by a state patrolman. Your throat tightens and you muster up the strength to get up and lumber back to the recovery room.

Eventually, the grief trigger passed, but it's sadly funny how your mind can focus and drift for so long just with the introduction of a reminiscent smell.

Some grief triggers can be positive, even bringing a smile to your face and solace in your heart. One such trigger was what to do with their mom's remains. The location of her ashes can always be a good reminder, but also a place to go and pay our respects, similar to that of a grave site.

The girls and I wore blue jeans and a white shirt that day, just like our last family photograph together, weeks before Lisa died. The four of us made the same trek in the car that we had made a hundred times from downtown to the beach. We all walked down to the ocean, feeling the white sand beneath our bare feet. I explained that their mom had been cremated and we could always come visit where we put her ashes. We had just left the church downtown and put a small plant shovel full of her ashes in the church garden, and her name was etched in the marble wall just above her resting place. The rest of her ashes would go into the ocean.

The ocean water was 45 degrees that day, the cold driving the force of what we were feeling even deeper. All three girls were squealing and saying, "No way." The cremated ashes had the consistency of light sand mixed with air. Each girl grabbed a handful of ashes and spread them on the beach. I rolled up my jeans and walked out into the ocean. Knee-deep, I placed the beautifully embroidered white laced box into the water. It was made with rice starch and supposed to dissolve quickly. The box floated peacefully on the water, and as I returned to shore, I thought that this was a brilliant idea, image, and metaphor for them to remember. We watched the box for a few minutes as it bobbed like a cork, and then a cold sweat came over me as the gentle wave brought the box back to our feet. Was the ocean too cold to melt the box? *Oh no*, I thought. *This was not a good idea.*

My oldest said, "Dad, I thought you said the box was going to melt and her ashes would dissolve in the ocean?" She spoke with audible caution.

"She doesn't want to leave us," the youngest said. A flash of light went through my head: my daughters were going to be scarred for life with the image of their mom's ashes motoring like a boat back to them.

"The water is really cold today," I said. "Let me try again."

Gently, I picked up the box and walked a bit further out, placing it again in the water.

As I walked to the shore, my middle daughter said, "Look, she liked it," as the box broke open. We watched together as a wave came and took the remaining ashes. With a great sigh of relief, I moved on to another day in my new life as a single parent.

CHAPTER XIX

Giving Up Control to the Universe

A FRIEND CAME UP TO ME IN THE COFFEE SHOP and started explaining that her cousin was terminally ill, but would not allow her to visit. She said her cousin was not acknowledging that she had a fatal, terminal disease and was dying. My friend asked me what she should do to help her cousin acknowledge the illness she was battling. For many suffering from a terminal illness, admission feels like giving up. We all have our unique experiences which form patterns or habits that are strong thoughts paved by neurochemicals down nerve roadways. Neurochemicals seek the path of least resistance every time. So, if yesterday you had a thought and today the neurochemical shows up at the same intersection, the neurochemical is inclined to flow down the same pathway and add a bit of pavement. Hence, a habit.

"I am lost," she said, "so what should I do to help her?"

I started out on a different tack.

"Okay, I have been driving for fifty years and have built habits in how I drive and where I park a car. This habit of fifty years is just one of the many we develop in our lifetimes. We get up, eat breakfast, go to work, come home, have a family, and do the same thing over and over again. So, let's apply this line of reasoning to your cousin who is not acknowledging her disease. What if I was driving your car, and when I started to park, you said, 'Hit this button and the car will park itself.' Watching the steering wheel turn itself as the car backed into a parking spot would be incredibly uncomfortable for me. Reflecting on my discomfort, I would realize that my habit was so engrained that I wouldn't be able to give in to the new technology and let the car do what is was engineered to do. My intuition wouldn't be to trust the car to park itself. I wouldn't be able to let the machine do something I had done so well for fifty years myself.

"My parking experience is probably how your cousin feels about acknowledging that she is dying. Her total denial is a life habit that will not let the machine of death do what it is supposed to do. There is not much you can do but be present with the person who is dying, as long as she allows it. Talk about the same things you normally would. Do not ignore it, just don't push it. Be present for her."

Processing grief can be even more traumatic if you are unable to accept the situation. Avoidance is not an answer; acceptance is not defeat. In our chaotic and controlling society, accepting death is perceived as giving up or giving into death, rather than giving up control. Loss is a natural part of living. Healthy acceptance of loss is a critical life skill in maintaining a balanced happiness.

Think about how our bodies deal with loss. If you cut yourself, your body sends chemicals to the cut to form blood clots to stop the bleeding. Shortly after that, your body starts to form a scab in order to heal the cut. In time, the scab flakes off to reveal a healthy layer of new skin. Over time, this leads to repairing the wound. Sometimes there is a little scar that serves as a reminder that you injured yourself. When looking at the scar, healthy people will generally remember with a smile the silly event that precipitated the cut. It is a normal trial and tribulation in life. We accept it and move on all the wiser.

So, what if a mental wound does not repair itself after a grief-related cut? Living with grief is not a habit that we practice until it happens to us. Our minds, thoughts, and actions are so dynamic and varied that processing grief is affected by our prior thoughts, experiences, and the environment of friends. Not processing grief is akin to no blood clots forming after a cut. If there are no mental scabs, how do you heal and move forward? Are you stuck, mentally hemorrhaging to death?

Outwardly, the frozen impairment of not forming a mental scab in response to a grief-cut could be expressed as anxiety, depression, self-harm, addiction, or other behaviors. A key to processing grief is to give up control of your life. You lost something, but even before that loss happened, none of us ever really have full control of our lives to begin with.

I remember giving up control to the universe and taking the role of a passenger, rather than the driver. All of my life I have felt in control, pushing to accomplish hard things. I worked my way through college and have been steadily working since. After Lisa passed, I stopped pushing as hard. While this sounds bad, it was actually a really liberating experience, and a sense of calm washed over me. To forage alone in life and spread happiness to those I encounter may be my calling. I recalled one of the last lines from *The Prince of Tides*: "I am a fourth grade teacher, and that is okay."

And then a remarkable thing happened. The sun started shining again, and I found the silver lining. It came to me in the form of a friend's friend. One day at the beach, I was talking with a friend of thirty years about the tragedy of dating as a fifty-something. I was putting what I wanted into the universe by talking with her and didn't even realize I was doing it.

"It'd be great to find someone who is somewhat normal, interested in traveling, likes food and wine, and laughs a lot." My friend of thirty years did not say anything to me but called her friend that night.

A few weeks later I met her friend, Susanna, and it was instantaneous. She is brilliant, attractive, and incredibly kind. We are true soulmates and are present with each other every day. Our families have come together for the benefit of all seven of us.

As you can see, the silver lining is that our families have been given a great gift—rebirth of living a purposeful, present life—A Beautiful Life. What a gift to experience, twice in one lifetime.

CHAPTER XX

Anger in Grief

AS A SURVIVOR, IT SEEMS SELFISH TO TALK ABOUT ANGER.
I was rarely angry before and am rarely angry today. In the first few months, and even today ten years later, many people ask or tell me about the stages of grief and mostly seem to focus on anger. Throughout the years, I have always had a great appreciation for life and been able to manage frustrations as they came along. Throughout my twenty-three-year marriage with Lisa, we had no regrets. At the end of every day we always cleared the deck with any issues we were facing. We argued fairly and always settled our differences amicably. That we had no regrets throughout our relationship was a tremendous asset during the most traumatic forty-two days of our lives. We were able to focus on each other rather than the things left unsaid or undone.

The anger I felt was at other people's actions and comments toward the girls. I felt annoyance, exasperation, impatience, irritation, and outrage at the things people said and did. The trauma of grief affected my personal demeanor, and I am sure I could have handled it better. I was less tolerant, less patient, and less considerate than I'd been before her passing. Fatigue and continuing layers of emotions filled up my emotional bucket. Reflecting back, I wish I had allowed myself more time to stop and think about what I'd say next when the frustrations started building up to an intolerable level. Thinking and saying things that deferred time, such as *I will give that good consideration*, or *I will think about it*, or *I appreciate what you are saying*. All of those responses would have been better than getting angry, but I have always been direct and honest about how I'm feeling in the immediacy of a moment. It was hard under the stress and pressure to be something different than I had always been.

Mindfulness helped me regain control of my ship and reverse the tension of anger. Focusing less on what words people said, and quietly listening to what was more important. Focusing on how to be present, respectful, and to enjoy each day helped me get back to my balanced mindset. Pausing, clearing my mind, and listening to thoughts that weren't grounded in anger helped me regain prior perspective.

There was a day in particular where I was reminded of the antithesis of anger. It was one of the most moving displays of love I have ever witnessed. I was a nineteen-year-old ambulance driver. I rolled into the emergency room as usual with a patient and entered him into the log in register. I happened to catch a glimpse of the couple in the next room. They were about eighty-five years old. She stood next to the bed holding her husband's hand attentively. "Can I do anything for you?" I asked.

"No, we're fine," she replied. "He had a heart attack a few hours ago after a fall. We have been married sixty-five years." It was a beautiful sight, seeing that marriage celebrated one last time. I had no idea then what a gift they had given me to enjoy every day of a partnership, a marriage a life. A subconscious piece of the puzzle, of who I wanted to be throughout my life, played out in front of me. Thirty years later, that memory helped provide perspective for some of the anxiety and frustrations I experienced with the sudden passing of my wife of 23 years and helped me give up control to the greater universe.

That my experience with the stages of grief were very different from what everyone expected has always bothered me a bit, as I was the one going through the trauma. In college I studied the Kubler-Ross Stages of Grief: Denial, Anger, Bargaining, Depression, and Acceptance. It made sense then and was a tidy model of an unthinkable experience. Even today, discrete prescribed stages of grief are so accepted in the world that some labeled my actions as inappropriate, that I was in denial, or that I had unresolved anger. Reactions ranged from *You did not focus on the girls enough*, to *You should not have done that*, to *You started dating too early*, and so on...These were all labeled as inappropriate, or mistakes because of grief.

My actions being labeled as "inappropriate grieving" felt wrong to me, then and now. As I went back and reread the stages of grief, a light bulb went off. Kubler-Ross's research was all done on terminal patients, and her assumption was that the families would follow the same process and pattern as with the dying patient. Based on my own experiences, that assumption seems biased and flawed. Grieving is just not that sequential, orderly, or tidy. Grieving is highly individualized, messy, emotional, and variable; each person has their own undefined timeline.

The Stevens Theory of Grief says that stages of grief are an inappropriate construct. Grief processing is more like a series of Venn diagrams rather than discrete stages. The circles are comprised of:

- Optimism of griever
- Resilience of griever
- Pace of processing of the griever
- Happiness of griever

Think about these key layers of behavior: optimism, resilience, pace of processing, and happiness. There may be other overlapping circles unique to each person, but successful grieving is about finding a personal flow of life. For whatever reason, faster grievers seem to have all of the circles fairly lined up, overlapped, and balanced. Protracted grievers have a higher variability of each characteristic, which overlaps grief in smaller amounts. The degree of overlap defines the time required to process grief. The greater the overlap, the faster the grieving proceeds, and the less overlap, the longer it takes to process grief. The grief process seems more three-dimensional than two-dimensional.

Fast Grieving

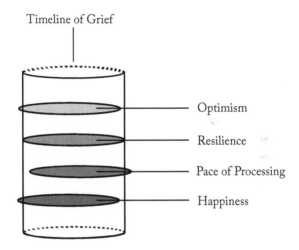

Slow Grieving

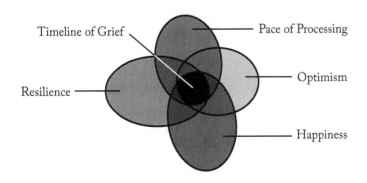

CHAPTER XXI

Guilt in Grief

GUILT IS A CLOSE RELATIVE OF ANXIETY, aggravating the already negative feelings that the grieving family is facing. Grief and guilt are both situational, in that a traumatic event causes grief, while something we say or do may cause us to feel guilty. Guilt can complicate the way we process grief, and negatively affect the important relationships in our lives—family, friends, or otherwise.

Some people feel guilty for being happy when a close friend is grieving. Hence the slow and awkward, "So, how are you doing?" Some parents will feel guilty being happy with their children when a friend has recently lost a child. How refreshing it was to hear, "I am sorry for your loss; I don't know what to say" or "I don't know how to help you and the girls in this unimaginable time, but know that I'm here if you need anything."

Some people feel guilty if they think they didn't do enough for a child who has passed. They may focus on the things left undone, unsaid, and unresolved. However, it is my belief that most parents are doing the best they can with what they have. Grieving parents will likely blame themselves for different reasons, with *could haves* and *should haves* running rampant through their minds. Shifting that negative internal chatterbox from past things left undone to positive memories can help. How rich we are with great memories for the time we did have together.

Some spouses feel guilty, wondering in the aftermath of a loss if they could have been better partners. Family members may also feel guilty in the midst of losing a loved one. They might think that they didn't help enough, or they didn't do this or that right. Rose still feels unwarranted shame for laughing when I told her her mom had cancer, and then again at the end of the funeral service, even after I reminded her that we all laughed when "You Can't Always Get What You Want" by the Rolling Stones came on. Rose's reactions were normal for a nine-year-old, and so it is easy to forget from a parent's perspective how the memory of her laughing could have such a lasting impact on her, causing increased shame and guilt. People of all ages struggle with guilt, particularly when grief is involved.

My good friend Will was telling me a story about how his father had a stroke and lived a decade before being diagnosed with Stage IV cancer with a six-month prognosis. He described how in those last six months, he wrote his father a letter thanking him for being such a great parent, community member, and role model, and that he would try to emulate his father's character. As you can imagine, it was extremely emotional for him to write. When he delivered it to his father, he expected him to read it. Instead, he asked if Will could read it for him, as his eyesight was failing. Will was not prepared to read the letter, as he had just stopped crying about writing it the night before. He sat by the hospital bed and opened the letter. He knew the only way he could get through the entire thing was to read it as if it was someone else's. He read it in a flat, monotone voice, bordering on disinterested; it was the only way he could get through it. His father was greatly appreciative, and they shared a special moment.

"So, what are you feeling guilty about?" I asked.

He said, "I feel guilty because I could not read the letter like I wanted to, nor could I convey my true appreciation and emotions to my father."

I understand the type of frustration that comes with regret. While I was not in the room with my friend twenty-two years ago, I am sure his father heard and understood. I am sure he heard the words of heartfelt conviction and understood how much his son loved him. I am sure Will's father could rest peacefully, seeing his character alive in his son. Banish the guilt of twenty-two years and think about the brilliance of that letter chronicling a beautiful life.

A key life preserver (or psychological tool) that helps reconcile and process emotions associated with grief is to recognize the thoughts when they present themselves and rescript the doubt component of guilt. Meaning, work on changing your *should haves* and *could haves* to *I did this* and *I also did that*. For example, I often feel guilty because I traveled a lot for work and was not home enough to be a great parent. However, instead of dwelling in that guilt, I try to follow that line of thinking with a positive affirmation. Yes, I traveled a lot for work and missed some great parenting opportunities, but when I was home, I was present and engaged. I took the kids on trips, attended every game they were involved in, cooked breakfast in the mornings, took them to school, and made every day with them as fun as I possibly could.

The key point is this: If you can subtly encourage the grieving person to rescript negative thoughts by replacing them with positive memories, it can help them process grief in a way that is both healthy and productive. You can incorporate the positive memory into the ongoing flow of your discussion without it feeling forced or awkward: *Hey, that reminds me of the time you did that crazy painting with your daughter. How much fun was that?*

Of course, as previously discussed, just being present is helpful. "I don't know what to say, but I'm here for you whenever you want to talk," is still one of the best things you can say to a person who is grieving.

It may sound manipulative, but it is important to get grieving parents to talk about their other children, focusing on what the surviving siblings are thinking and feeling, and how the parents plan on helping them through this incredibly difficult time period. This simple question will reposition the parent's role in the situation, from a grieving parent to a parent working with grieving children. This change of focus helps the parent fight through grief, and gives the siblings solace as well. It is not avoiding grief but modeling how to handle it in a proportional manor.

Will called the other day, struggling with how to talk to his eighteen-year-old son. His son recently lost a close friend that he had taken to prom. She passed away suddenly in an accident. Will's question was, "What should I say to him? Do I talk about what he is thinking? Do I sympathize with him or what?" And then he said the most amazing thing: "It's a funny coincidence that just the other day, I was thinking of my close school friend, Sallie, who died in a car accident when I was eighteen. That was almost forty years ago now, but I still occasionally think of her."

I asked him, "What thoughts do you have about Sallie?"

Will paused and said, "I remember her laugh like it was yesterday. I still get the biggest smile when I think of the fun times we had and her infectious laugh."

"Have you shared that story with your son?" I asked.

"No," he replied.

"Share that story with him, just like you did with me, and ask him what he thinks he will remember most about his friend. It's a great opportunity for both of you, to solidify a positive memory together, and share common father-son experiences; it'll provide great parental modeling to an eighteen-year-old on how to handle grief for the rest of his life."

He did and it has.

CHAPTER XXII

Consider Practicing These Questions Before Talking to a Grieving Friend

WE ALL SEEM TO PRACTICE BEFORE WE DO THINGS that are important to us. We practice sports before games, we practice our instruments before playing music, and we study before a test, but we do not practice what we are going to say to a friend who has just experienced losing someone they loved. We should.

Before talking to someone dealing with grief, consider reading these questions and trying to answer them. If you like what you see in the mirror, charge forward. If not, take a moment and spend some time thinking about what you really want to say. You will do a great favor to your friend in need.

- What do I need to know about my grieving friend?
- How do I help my friend and their family in this situation?
- How do I deal with my own grief for the family in this situation?
- How should I act around the family?
- How do I keep from adding my grief to their burden?
- What specifically should I say and not say to the adults and children?
- What should I do and not do in this situation?
- What is important to the family right now?
- How can I help the family's friends deal with grief?
- What can be done quietly for the family without asking?

- What does the future look like without this person in our lives?
- What role am I willing to take in the healing process? Active, passive, or none?
- Is all grief created equal? Accidental, illness, expected, or sudden?
- What would I want someone to do or say if I were in the griever's shoes?
- What would I want to talk about?
- What would I not want to talk about?
- What environment would be most comfortable for my friend? A coffee shop, their house, my house, or somewhere else?
- How can I be most helpful to my friend?
- What do I want out of the interaction? To help, express my feelings, or something else?
- Should I talk with our peer group about this?

CHAPTER XXIII

Friends of Children

TEENAGE GIRLS CAN BE BRUTAL to each other. They can cut deeper with words than a butcher knife. We all know one or ten. It is hard to understand how these sweet eleven-year-olds can suddenly derive satisfaction from controlling, bullying, and oppressing. We all know them; they go for the kill when they smell weakness. And so it was with my grief-stricken daughter.

There was no yard pass for losing your mother. Some of her best friends would vie for her undivided attention, and when that didn't work, the seemingly nice girls would bully her for domination. One said, "You should only be my friend, because H said so and so" or "If you are my best friend, then you cannot be her friend." As a father watching my youngest struggling with the trauma and pain of loss, I wanted to strangle the little twits. But such is life. We've all seen it and see it in our offices and workplaces today. I tried to talk with each of the girls to explain on several occasions what was really going on, but they struggled to understand.

Talk with your children to try and help prepare them for the awkwardness of their friends trying to talk about death. Their peers will simply not know what to say, which injects an unintended callousness into the interaction. Some will very appropriately say *I am sorry about your mom*. One of the most considerate responses came from Lillie, a thirteen-year-old friend of my middle daughter, who said, "I don't know what to say, but if you want to talk about it, I'm here for you."

Many comments will not be clear or understandable to grieving children, but some preparation is better for them than none. Providing grieving young children with a few words they can say will give them a tool or two to use with their group of friends. Guiding friends of young children who are grieving to use words like kindness, understanding, friendship, and helpful will convey compassion and empathy for their friend's predicament.

CHAPTER XXIV

Friends of Adults

STRESSFUL TIMES DO NOT BUILD CHARACTER—they bring it out.

It is remarkably rewarding (and sometimes disappointing) to learn the content of a friend's character. It highlights what was already there but was difficult to discern. The friends you were sure would be there may not stick around. And the ones you did not think about being there will be. Learn from it. Surround yourself with positive influences. If a friend is negative, it is not a reflection on you, but a reflection on their character. We all know one or two, the people that talk negatively about people, cutting and criticizing everything from dress to embarrassing situations to comments out of context. Some people just live for the negative reinforcement of drama. At this stressful time in your life, it is best to minimize exposure to the negative relationships, to protect your mental health and peace of mind. True friends will be there. Don't lose sleep over the ones who aren't.

We are not always aware of why we associate with different people or a certain group of friends. For example, one friend told me they are more likely to befriend other couples with children in the same age group. It is convenient and logical, but may not be the most beneficial or personally rewarding situation.

People have their own agenda—for better or for worse—and will say things that highlight their character, be it positive or negative. It is a true window into their relationships, lives, frustrations, and anxieties, but projected onto you—your situation and relationships. Judgment seems to be an easy go-to for some folks. The discussion might start out with your friend saying, *You should be doing this,* or *You need to be focusing on that,* or *Things would be better if you just did this.*

On the other side of the ledger is full continuum with friends like Jane. She was staying with us at our home when Lisa was dying. One day, right after Lisa was given more morphine, Jane—my wife's college roommate—came into the room and sat on her bed. Jane was a social worker living in Maine dealing with distressed families. She had several years' worth of experience dealing with unfortunate calamities in the lives of people in her community, but none as close to her and her personal life. I called Jane myself to let her know what was happening, but had to leave a voicemail. She called back and left a message saying that maybe she would wait until after Christmas to visit, respecting our privacy and waiting for the dust to settle.

I returned her call and left a voicemail in response: "I am sorry to leave this in a voicemail, but if you want to see your college roomie, you need to come this week or next."

She called back crying and came the next day. I made dozens of those calls, as many people seem to think all cancers have a prognosis defined in years, and are something to live with and work around. Jane is a kind, sweet soul who listened attentively as we described what we were doing with the videos, pictures, and lockets. It was a bittersweet scene of old friends saying goodbye at the young age of forty-six.

These silent angels will quietly be there when you need them, and do things for you and your family without you even having to ask. Once in a while you find a quarter face up (meaning twenty-five days of good luck), or someone smiles, or lets you merge in a long line of traffic, or asks you how you are doing and really means it. And then there are those life-changing, staggering moments when someone steps up to the plate in the moment you need them the most. I experienced such a moment with Jane, and then again with another friend, Allison.

Allison is a low-key person with a colossal heart. In the days after Lisa's death, she quietly did things for us around the house, whether it was emptying the garbage, running an errand, or just offering a comforting smile. She is defined by her strength and beautiful character. In my case, she was our good family friend, a stalwart amongst us. She displayed incredible strength and presence during those 42 days. I have seen her periodically but less than I would like in the last few years and have come to understand from her that ten years later, she has still not come to terms with Lisa's passing.

Other silent angels included, my good friend Will, who delivered a load of firewood and stacked it so we could have a soothing fire every night. John orchestrated installing a hot tub. Jim repaired a door that was broken. Jane brought over a crocheted blanket for the girls. Karen organized delivery of three meals a week for months. Jackson asked me to go on a boy's ski trip with him. Hugh, someone I did not know very well, said he was there if I needed anything. Many other friends were available and willing to talk when I needed it the most. Elizabeth brought over a book her husband asked her to drop off. She had the remarkable presence to sit on the front porch with me, talking about nothing. It was a heavenly break from the ongoing presence of grief. For five glorious minutes we sat shoulder to shoulder, talking about nothing. For a moment in my new life, I was normal again.

CHAPTER XXV

The Good, the Bad, and the Ugly: Things People Say to Grieving Children and Adults

GET READY FOR IT, because it is one of the few things I can guarantee. People will say the most unusual things in the most unusual ways at the most inopportune times. It is primarily because they don't know what to say, and so they force something out.

If I could give friends only one piece of advice it would be WAIT. WAIT is my acronym for Why Am I Talking? Silence can also be useful to someone who just experienced loss. Just be present with your grieving friend. Don't talk to fill up the room. Under intense stress, many people's filters slip, releasing some of their most unappealing thoughts: judgment, piety, and hypocrisy, which seem to flourish in this sad environment, much like mildew in a wet basement. Some people are responding not to who you are today, but to their perception of how you were in the past. While it is hard to understand or believe, more than half of your relationships and friendships will likely change in a very short period of time. Some people will be busy or traveling or have parental obligations, and that is okay.

Even some of your closest friends will struggle. After all, yesterday you were part of a couple and today you are not. Becoming a single person again can unsettle many important relationships.

I was startled by so many of the comments my daughters and I received, most especially from those based on what my wife supposedly once said. Some of the more challenging ones were:

- Your wife/mother is in a better place.
- We all seek to walk with God, and I wish I were there with Lisa.
- Your wife was so important to so many people; you must give everyone else a chance to adjust to your fast pace of grieving.
- We may never get over her loss.
- You are ostracizing your friends (particularly the moms) by treating your children this way (parenting the same way as I had before, with a fairly strict hand).
- Your wife would want this to happen this way.
- Your wife would want us to be together. (Really?)
- I promised your wife I would help the kids grow up.
- I promised your wife I would help the kids in high school.
- How are you doing?
- How are the girls doing?

This last question requires a bit of thinking, as it seems innocuous but had a larger-than-expected influence in our experience. I was driving the car one day (Nadir plus 155 days) with all three of my girls, when my ten-year-old daughter brought up an interesting topic.

She said, "Dad, people say the funniest things to us. Adults especially. They'll say, 'How are you doing?'" Her adult voice was funny, a tone that was deep and slow. "And when I say I'm doing fine in school, they talk slower and say, 'No, no, no, how are you *really* doing?' It's like they're on a different page of the story than we are. We're on page ninety-nine, and they're on page nine." Out of the mind of a ten-year-old—it was that simple.

From day one to ten years later, we still get the same question in the same somber tone: "How are the girls doing?" I may be a bit oversensitive, but it seems to be a question that is not the same as, "Tell me what the girls are up to?" It just comes off as, "How are the girls living with the death of their mother?" The problem with this is that they're focused on the wrong thing. The girls' ability to move on isn't discounting Lisa's memory, but honoring her in a different way: through the success of her children growing up and continuing to contribute to society. Defining children by an event such as their mother's traumatic death detracts from their individuality and demeans the success of each child. Sometimes it seems as though certain people have a permanent label affixed to my daughters that reads *The Three Sisters Whose Mother Died*, rather than the three bright and well-adjusted girls who contribute to society.

Children do not want to be defined by the death of a parent.

To this day, I continue to get text messages from two good friends, one male and one female, twice a year. One on Lisa's birthday, and one on her death day. These are two of the kindest people on the planet. Their texts explain how much they miss Lisa, and how they are thinking about her on those days, too. For the first year or two, I thought it was kind and considerate. After ten years, I worry they may not have processed their grief. I want to think that they are celebrating her life and their memories, but that is not how it seems.

Unintentionally, some friends can sometimes make your life more difficult and intense during this stressful period of time. One year after my wife died, I felt compelled to send a letter to a good friend to say enough was enough. His anger and grief had been turned to focus on me instead. After a series of very negative phone calls filled with backseat driving and second-guessing, I had to tell him how toxic I found his treatment of me. It was clear that some friends were slow to process grief, because they did not think about it every day as the family is forced to do. It was a turning point for me, as I had dealt with all of the negatives from many different directions without becoming angry. The cumulative effect of a longtime friend suddenly becoming hostile pushed me over the edge.

I tried to communicate what I had learned about grief and relationships in the last year, and in particular to my friend's expectations of people's responses. My message was simple. Do not be disappointed with the response of bereaved friends; there is nothing positive to come from focusing on their response.

It seemed important to others to make sure that I was in counseling as well as the kids. While I had been going to counseling, my friends had not. There was a big gap in what people were thinking, how they were processing their emotions, and how we were processing ours. Everyone was in enormous pain from the loss of a lovely person, but the result was expressing judgment in regards to how my daughters and I chose to grieve.

Grieving families: you must focus on what you need to do for each other and what will be helpful from your perspective in dealing with friends' unprocessed grief, as well as their inability to cope. What some friends seemed to want for me was that in three or four years after a long mourning period and no dating I might meet someone. Even then there would be questions, comments. It is human nature and our friends are human. While I do not agree with the highly judgmental nature of some people's comments, I do understand it, and most are years away from coping. But in the letter to my college friend, I wrote:

"Allow me the courtesy of getting on my high horse for one minute. I have been here 24 hours every day for 365 days, each year with each girl, with whatever it is they need. Driving Charlotte to school at 7:00 a.m., dropping off June at the orthodontist at 8:00 a.m., picking up Rose at Cotillion at 7:00 p.m., making breakfast before school every morning, dinner every night, making sure the house stays clean, ensuring all three girls have clean laundry, listening to drama from fifth-grade, eighth-grade, and eleventh-grade girls, and making sure each holiday and birthday is perfect, all so I can provide great consistency and stability for my children. What gives my friends the moral high ground to judge how I am doing things?"

I continued to explain my experiences and feelings.

"True friends support each other, not question them. True friends ask what they need, rather than decide for them. True friends take the initiative instead of shying away. Why not seek to support me in my next chapter, not obstruct or undermine it? In the last year, I have processed a minimum of 8,760 thoughts of grief to everyone else's 52. At this rate, it'll be 168.46 years before everyone else catches up."

There was little consideration as to how I felt or what the girls really needed. This note to my friend might sound angry, but it's more complicated than that. It was an expression of disbelief and frustration with a friend I'd had since college, during a time we needed him the most. The letter did not bring about change. After more of the same, our friendship ended.

Is it possible they are so blocked by grief that they are no longer being themselves? The message here is, unfortunately, a disappointing one. It will not be hard to figure out who your supportive friends are after a life-changing event, but it will be hard to face who is not. In the years following a death, more than half of your friends will likely change. Many of your friends came to know you as a couple, went to parties you attended as part of a couple, talked with you as a couple, and now—without your significant other— you no longer fit their profile. It isn't as crass as it sounds, but it is human behavior. Some people just aren't equipped to handle change, and don't know how to process the conflict of new emotions built on a history they're used to.

We lived across the street from our great friend and oncologist. He met me in the middle of the street at midnight one unseasonably warm evening, both of us standing in T-shirts and boxer shorts. He explained that this is a behavior he has seen over and over again in his practice. He warned that some of Lisa's close friends would not want to move forward in the grieving process.

"In a weird way," he said, "they are grasping at something that makes them feel alive. In the midst of a mid-life crisis, mid-40s, with kids and routine jobs, no excitement prevails. And then something tragic and unexplainable happens, so wrought with emotion, and it is the most alive they've felt in a decade. So they can't let go, they can't move forward. Many of the experiences you described highlight the fact that some people want to perpetuate and feed on the feelings and emotions they are sensing in you, because they don't feel with such intensity anymore. Their daily lives are too unfulfilled, unfocused, or just empty. Your loss adds something exciting to their lives."

His description was unimaginable to me at the time, but the more I experienced it, the more real it became. It is the pornography of grief.

Clyde Edgerton, a brilliant writer, once said of parenting and in-laws in his book *Pappdaddy's Book for New Fathers: Advice to Dads of All Ages*, "If they are dead, your in-laws will probably not interfere with your fathering. But they may be…whispering in your wife's ear." I can verify that observation and confirm that, after death, they will be coming to you directly.

When your relatives overstep their boundaries, you may start to define a new relationship with them. You may find that family members of the one who died make the loss harder for you in your grief. After excruciating months of comments, barbs, calls, and peer pressure, I decided to write a letter to express my concerns, feelings, and thoughts. I tried to establish factual details of what actions we were taking to help us in our healing. Part of the letter read:

ooooo

"I would like to help you help all of us. Rose, June, and Charlotte are happy and doing very well, as am I. We are all dealing with our tragedy in our own way, but are choosing to be happy. This decision does not degrade or insult Lisa's legacy—it exemplifies and celebrates it. We changed therapists over the summer with fabulous results. The first therapist had a "tell me how you really feel" approach, which did not help any of us process our grief, only revisit it. Our new therapist is remarkable. She challenges our thoughts and feelings and does not hesitate to call us out for our BS when we're wallowing in grief.

"I do not expect you to support me 100 percent. I would, however, challenge you to be more focused on healing the impossible wound this has left you with, adding value where you can, and minimizing activities that do not add to that value. As I deal with single parenting—getting the kids up and fed before school, my own career, doctors and dentist appointments, after school activities, my mother's health, my sister's antics, and all that our lives entail—addressing your grief would help us with ours.

"So, I am teaching my children and using myself as an example to live in the moment and not wait for the rest of our lives. Plan for tomorrow, respect the past, but live your life today. You and others have judged this as selfish, and I can no longer live with that. I have often felt that many people in our lives would be more comfortable if my family was paralyzed by grief, unhappy and unable to move forward. But I know Lisa would not want that for us. I have drawn on every ounce of energy, will, courage, strength, and pure gut instincts to rise beyond my grief and move forward, in order to be an example for my children. I have to make sure that we live, because it was Lisa who told me that's what she wanted."

One of the key things I hoped to accomplish was to outline what was helping me at the time and what was not. You might know these things, but may feel powerless to explain it to your relatives. Tell them without hesitation.

Things that add value and are helpful for the Stevens family:

- Supportive relatives
- Supporting the father
- Supporting the children
- Talking about Lisa at appropriate moments only
- Supporting the new family and the environment we worked to create

Unfortunately, the result of this email involved several of our relatives and friends calling me to explain how wrong I was, and how I should handle the stress better. Looking back ten years the wiser, I am sure I could have handled it differently, but I am not sure if anything would have changed the outcome in regards to their response. It seemed that no matter what course of action I took in my grief, they were always going to tell me how I should have handled it better, and what they would have done instead.

CHAPTER XXVI

A Consequence of Unresolved Grief

I AM NOT A GRIEF EXPERT. Rather, I am experienced at grieving.

I have been thrown into the grief pool many times, and have watched the small and large ripples of emotional waves circle away from me and around my life. Just when you thought the waves of anguish were subsiding, they bounced off the side of some distant wall, and returned to you like a boomerang, just to rock the boat. The many facets of my loss and grief include: my parents' divorce when I was eleven years old, my father's death when I was twenty-nine years old, my grandmother's death at thirty-two years old, the death of a close friend and mother of three at forty years old, my spouse of twenty-three years and the mother of our three happy girls at forty-seven years old, a close personal friend who died when I was fifty-three, and my mother's death at fifty-five. Not even these experiences and learnings were enough to prepare me for the loss of my youngest daughter.

As a parent I always talked with the girls about the consequences of their actions, good and bad. Each of our individual actions has a consequence for something or someone. It felt like an easy parenting tool. When they did something good, the consequence was a reward: praise, ice cream, or an outfit for their favorite doll. When they did something that was not acceptable, the consequence was punishment: being grounded, getting their cell phone taken away for the week, or cleaning the bathrooms for everyone (which they particularly disliked). The situations were usually easy to spot—a rule broken or followed, cleaning up their rooms on time with a smile, or breaking a dish in frustration.

It did not occur to me how this was not as easily applicable to grief, or the magnitude of pain that unresolved grief could inflict. It was a consequence of inaction.

This is a particularly difficult part of this story, but I sincerely believe in its importance to share. Three girls at three different ages, who grew up in the same environment, handled the grievous shock of losing their mother in different ways. Whether the youngest would have taken the same path regardless of her mother's sudden death is arguable, but at its minimum, it disproportionally destabilized her at a crucial juncture in life's developmental pathway. It is possible that the combined experience she had pushed her off the diving board into the deep end of the self-destructive cesspool.

By sharing these extraordinarily painful and sensitive experiences, we hope to stay on the topic of grief but provide context of other pathways that unresolved grief can lead to.

It was a regular hectic night in 2015, three days before Christmas. Susanna and I were in the kitchen cooking dinner, and our twenty-two-year-old was home from her senior year of college. The three of us were drinking red wine and barking about senior year, job hunting, and life after college. It was about 5:00 p.m. when I asked June to go check on her sister again, to drag her downstairs for our pre-Christmas merriment.

"Dad," she said, "I checked on her about an hour ago, and she was cranky and out of it. How about you try?"

"You're right, June. It's time for me to be the Disciplinarian Dad one more time!"

I put my wine down and bounced up the stairs to her room.

"Rose, come join us downstairs. We are cooking…"

I immediately noticed her face was glazed over, mumbling something I couldn't understand. She was leaning with her head bent over the top of the mattress, in an awkward position against the wall. It didn't make sense. I sat on the bed and stroked her head.

"Rose, come downstairs with us and cook dinner." I noticed a green color on the wall that looked like one of those crazy frozen drinks. "Rose, what did you spill?"

And then my life changed forever.

"Rose, there are two bottles of pills here with the caps off and empty. Did you take any?" I said. I tried to keep my voice as calm as I possibly could.

"Yes," she replied, voice garbled.

"How many?" I asked.

"All of them," she said.

I quickly grabbed the bottles: Adderall 20 mg, 30 tablets; Zoloft 20mg, 90 tablets; one bottle of Advil. I talked loudly and slowly, trying to figure out how many pills she had swallowed. It took everything in me not to ask *Why*.

I screamed down to Susanna and June: "Come up here now!"

After seeing Rose and the empty bottles, Susanna acted immediately: "I'll call 911."

My sweet eighteen-year-old daughter had used her fingernails to scratch in a white painted chest of drawers beside her bed, "I want to go visit Mommy."

The first responders arrived in minutes, asked a lot of questions about our family, and took her to the emergency room.

We showed up in the ED about 8:30 p.m. *Monday Night Football* was going on in the background, and normal life inched along for everyone but us. We sat in the hallway of the crowed ED looking at each other, stunned. She was dazed from the large quantity of drugs coursing through her veins; I was dazed that I could be participating in this train wreck. *Are we really in the ED? Did my daughter really just try to kill herself?* She knew how I despised that demon, suicide and its sibling, depression. I am a rescuer. I help everyone, for as long as I could remember. It's what I do.

At 3:00 a.m. in any emergency room you will see the full spectrum of Americana. All facets, ages, and personalities. Drained from reason and filled with both anxiety and fatigue, I started thinking about the paths that got me there. How long had it been? It was December 2015, and Lisa passed in November of 2005. Had it really been ten years since my life was thrown into turmoil? Had it really been ten years since I got the call? Had it really been ten years since that life-changing event?

"Sir." The nurse had to shake me to snap out of my trance. After excruciating hours of self-doubt, criticism, shame, and regret, of asking myself over and over, *What could I have done differently?*

Doctors and nurses came, and went with little regard for either of us. The island got smaller and the boat further away. Finally, one doctor came by and said she would be okay, but they had to screen for psychiatric risks, and she would be transferring to 4 South for a few days of observation.

It was two days before Christmas as I walked into the hospital's entrance, unsure about what came next. Walking faster than usual, I turned the corner to the elevator and spotted a friendly face. Dan was a psychiatrist and oncologist; he always covered the week of Christmas. We'd shared meals together and talked about common interests, usually in psychology, medicine, and cancer detection. I saw a smile cross his face, then immediately melt away as he read mine. "Where are you headed?" he asked.

4 South.

Dan was such a kind soul, and always made it easy to open up to him. We talked about death, loss, kids, and what came next. We exchanged some ideas, but the fatigue of spending all night in the emergency room got the best of me. It was nice seeing a friend before I headed to the unknown lands of 4 South—the psych ward.

The elevator was restricted going to 4 South, with an attendant at the door as I exited. "How can I help you?" she asked.

Each ward in the hospital had a unique characteristic. Cardiovascular floors have the incessant beeping of heart monitors in every room, and warnings going off in the nursing station. OB/GYN floors carry a cloud of tension. Pediatric wards are quiet and heavy with nervous parents facing uncertainty, while trying to pretend for their children that everything is okay. Orthopedic floors have a lot of grunting and groaning, as patients try to walk or stretch after serious surgery. Geriatric floors are quiet with reflection, and families worried about mom or dad. All floors are busy with activity and emotion.

Psych wards are different. There is an artificial quietness in the air with small sitting areas. Every bedroom door stays open. The TV is always on and most patients are medicated. There are no crash carts or bandage stations, but the fear of losing a patient is just as great on any other hospital floor. The wounds and scars are not obvious, but it doesn't mean they aren't there. Like cardiovascular problems, they can be deceptively hidden or slow nagging pains. Whether angina or anxiety, high blood pressure or depression, atrial fibrillation or psychosis—the pain of their wounds is ubiquitous, and is written on each face in a very different language.

Mental health issues are not to be taken lightly. They are life-threatening, and tragedies unto themselves. In many cases, these illnesses have a direct connection to drug abuse, an attempt to quiet the underlying anxiety, depression, or whatever mental illness that person's struggling with. It is a sad truth in today's world that the face of your mother, father, sister, brother, friend, spouse, son, or daughter can be buried in the statistics that we all hear in the news. We used to gasp in disbelief that this kind of behavior was going on in our country. We ignored it instead of making it a national emergency. And now no one in this country can say that they don't know at least one person who is struggling with mental health issues.

My daughter's case manager walked into the room and asked me to come into her office. She had a kind but terse facial expression, and wild curly hair. She struck me as somewhere between super kind and super intense. Maybe it was how she survived working in a very challenging environment.

"Sir, have you ever had an experience like this?"

"No," I said.

"I want to help you get through this, but I need to ask you questions about your daughter and your family. Has she ever attempted suicide before?"

"No."

"Does she have anxiety issues?"

"Yes, she has text anxiety, and she always gets nervous as the center of attention. While she is extremely extroverted, she doesn't want more attention than she already gets; people really seem to gravitate to her."

"Has she ever been treated for depression?"

"Yes, at sixteen."

"Has she ever been molested?"

"No."

"Have you ever touched your daughter inappropriately?"

"WHAT? *No.*"

Looking back on this event—and the twenty-seven subsequent treatment facilities we experienced in the last five years—I realize now that most healthcare professionals are a bit prejudiced against the family. I'm sure it represents their cumulative experience—but not mine. It feels as though the default way of thinking is that the family abused the person, or pushed the person into suicide.

"Has the stepmom ever had an issue with your daughter?"

"What mom or stepmom hasn't had an issue with a hormonal teenager?"

"Sir, I need serious answers. Do you understand we are in a psychiatric ward? All of the folks here have severe mental health issues, and your daughter just attempted suicide. Do you understand the prevalence of mental illness in America? Your daughter checks off several boxes."

I believe mental health in the US, particularly in the last twenty years, is largely at the fault of our state and federal lawmakers, who lapsed into an era of disregard for mental health as a real condition. We do not take care of our citizens like other countries; we could do so much better...

"Sir, do you understand that 1 in 5 adults in the US experience mental illness in a given year, and among the 20 million adults in the US who experienced a substance use disorder, 50 percent have a co-occurring mental illness?"

"I knew it was a huge problem, but I didn't understand the magnitude of it here in the US, or that my daughter is one of the 20 million. Can we talk about her situation and what her best options are?"

"Well, more than 90 percent of people who die by suicide show symptoms of a mental health condition, so we should start with the underlying mental health issues that may have driven her to take this course of action."

"How can we focus on the specific granular issues that surround her at this minute, right here and right now? The air, the temperature, the lights—what can we do to help my daughter today?"

I did not know it then, but that was the day I lost the person I knew as my sweet eighteen-year-old daughter. I have faith and hope that she will return someday.

CHAPTER XXVII

Community and Connectivity

THE PARALLELS BETWEEN GRIEF and recovery from addiction are strikingly similar. The perception of addiction is that people are broken, lazy losers. Made famous by Nixon's war on drugs in 1971, this prejudice prevails today. Ironic that some of the most pious people were opioid addicts, like Joseph McCarthy for example. Ironic how, in the war on drugs, the patients are castigated, but one of Nixon's other wars, the war on cancer patients, are heroes battling the ultimate evil.

Grief exposes, aggravates, and amplifies unresolved issues, affecting those who struggle with mental health, anxiety, and depression. The road forward can be paved with positive or negative coping mechanisms. One path is to turn grief and loss into self-destructive behaviors, such as self-harm, overeating, purging, drugs, or alcohol. The need to dull the senses or feel numb seems immediate—anything to not feel pain. The hard part is that we all internalize and express things differently based on our personalities and experiences. We all have little voices on each shoulder with diametrically opposed views and beliefs, one positive and one negative, who both talk incessantly while seeking to dominate their foe on the other shoulder.

Sometimes they both sound negative, and when they team up it can drive abrupt changes in behavior. Some folks only hear the negative internal chatterbox, and it is a brutal self-critic. Many times, the expression or change in mental health looks the same as a normal brooding teenager. In the moment, the behavior is indistinguishable from the sweet little girl you know, but the resulting actions boil below the surface and are quite a different color.

One of the family recovery programs we participated in suggested that the word *trigger* is not a great word to describe the intense emotional feelings and stimulations, because it abdicates responsibility for being able to handle and deal with the feelings that many of us have. Learning how to deal with the intensity level and frequency of emotions is part of finding your way out of the situation that you're in. For me, a grief trigger was just that: a sudden unexpected shot out of the dark with the ability to expose emotional nerves in an instant.

Recovery, whether from drugs or from grief, requires rejuvenating some of the key foundations that anchor us all to the ground. There are many interesting parallels for this broader way of thinking. The recovering person must find new meaning in everyday life. When it comes to mental health, building a life worth living is the most important brick in the foundation of a new home. Seeking out and finding a healthy "tribe" is essential to successful recovery. However, finding said tribe can be difficult, since many people struggling with mental illness and addiction relapse along the way, creating risk within the group. A muffled brain signal seems to be telling them that these folks are the good guys, and everyone else in their earlier life was bad. Chasing this line of thinking is a risk for those trying to recover. Interactions with positive supporters (mentors, therapists, etc.) reinforce healthy behaviors, provide supportive friendships, solid networks, and demand honest accountability from your new life. It is a house that is built with one brick at a time.

One of the most unfortunate aspects of death is that it heightens many people's life experiences. For some people, it is (ironically) the most alive they have felt in years, and those people will want to swim in the grief and perpetuate it—not process it. Every friend group has a few willing participants, usually veiled as an abundance of concern for one particular child, or an overly protracted involvement in getting something special for someone. In reality, it's just fuel for their own personal drama. Recognize the situation, contain it if possible, and put them in the parking lot of your life. It is too draining on your limited emotional fuel.

The reality is that drug use is an escape in order to reduce emotional pain or get away from the underlying mental health issues. How is it that we do not help people who have a mental illness? We do not disparage people with cancer, heart disease, or other chronic illnesses as we do with mental health. It's time for a serious change in how our society talks about mental illness and addiction.

It seems that those struggling with addiction become disconnected from the key elements of life that keep us moving forward.

- Meaningful work
- Other people
- Community
- Meaningful values
- The ability to reconcile with childhood trauma
- Respect for oneself and others
- The natural world
- Hope for the future

Reconnect. Reconnecting with family, friends, and community is essential for moving forward in a healthy way. Starting with one small step that can lead to another is important for turning what we want from our lives into our new reality—a house that is built with one brick at a time.

- Find meaningful work
- Regain a sense of purpose
- Help others by volunteering for something
- Embrace people
- Find your community
- Show your true values
- Let go of whatever guilt or shame you may be feeling from past mistakes
- Do what brings you joy
- Feel that joy for others
- Accept empowerment

The value and importance of being connected to a community and the risk of being disconnected from your tribe or community has become clearer to me throughout this journey. Driving down the road with perfect 80-degree weather, I was listening to music and thinking about how I gave up control to the universe. Suddenly, an Amy Winehouse song came on the radio. Amy Winehouse had a beautiful voice, and an interrupted life. She died at twenty-seven of alcohol poisoning. The lyrics to "Rehab" resonated with me, as I immediately thought of my youngest daughter, Rose. It's frustrating to know that some people seem to think that those struggling with addiction must like their situation. Otherwise, why would they keep doing it?

It's the relief, or how they interpret that relief. Respite from their demons, numbness, some satisfaction, a high feeling from the release of endorphins, or chasing other targets that make them feel alive.

I have come to the opinion that addictive behaviors do not have to involve drugs. Some of the most broken people I have met are drama queens, narcissists, workaholics, etc., and they are not using drugs to obtain that feeling. Their high is a dose of dopamine or adrenaline from bullying someone, the thrill and rush of lying behind someone's back, the excitement from working twenty hours a day, or some other chemically dependent reward. Their addiction is the sensation they seek out through their varying behaviors. They may not want to do the deed, but want the satisfaction of the result.

The driving cause of this behavior is usually anxiety, depression, or anger. Anxiety and depression seem to have three origins: genetics, situational events, and social environments. A successful program to address unresolved issues must include and evaluate each possible cause. Each layer of the onion must be observed and gently peeled back to reveal the heart of the problem.

Since that first emergency room visit four years ago, a part of my subconscious had been waiting for the call. Unlike the other life changing call from Jack about Lisa in 2005, I had time to think about, obsess over, ruminate on, prepare for, and grieve through the expected next call. Like a broken record, it played hundreds of times—over and over and over again—dreading the horrible outcome.

My phone rings.

"Mr. Stevens, this is Officer Jones. Are you the father of a Rose Stevens?"

"Yes, I am."

"We located your number in her cell phone under Dad. Sir, I am sorry to inform you that your daughter has died. Will you be making arrangements to collect the body?"

Imagine expecting those words from every single call you received for the last four years. Imagine answering calls from random numbers, because the area code may be where your daughter was at that moment. Imagine the stress, anxiety, depression, guilt, and the bounty of other emotionally toxic ways of thinking that corrodes your normally positive personality. Imagine that stress being built on the responsibility of being a widower, which means you are the last warm blanket between security for your girls or leaving them as orphans in the world.

Addiction is miserable for the addict and the family. It took me almost two years into Rose's recovery to set healthy boundaries that I could live with. After all, if the worst happened, I needed to know that I had done everything possible to save my daughter's life. By spending tens of thousands of dollars out of pocket on different forms of recovery—detox, rehab, eating disorder facilities, therapists, and clinics—I finally realized with the help of Al-Anon that I was codependent, and only I could change that. Through a few agonizing days, I was able to get to the point where I no longer had to pay. She would go to facilities that accepted insurance only, and I would continue to provide a cell phone so she could work and have a lifeline.

Watching my daughter disintegrate in front of me felt like the last scene from *Titanic*, where Rose watched Jack slide under the surface of the water with his eyes still open, watched as he drifted to the bottom of the ocean.

It is heart break after heart break after heart break.

CHAPTER XXVIII

Photo Journal

AS ONE OF THE DOZENS OF LAST-DITCH EFFORTS to help Rose I thought our family photos and videos might remind her of the life she had and what she has to look forward to in life. I put a photo journal together and added captions. Envision a photo journal from your family's life. So many of us have images like the ones described below.

As you read this section, imagine your own family images and the life your family has lived.

Rose,

We love you and are scared. We want good things for you, but no one can do it for you. I know you remember how every Christmas we watched the movie *It's A Wonderful Life*. These pictures are of your wonderful life so far.

Life is a journey and you are the captain of your own ship. You are in control of your destiny although you may not feel like it. Your addiction is limiting your path to a great future, threatening your life, and is no longer sustainable. Drugs are warping your memories of the past and fueling your poor decisions. We are all sad.

You are the only one who can change this.

Please think about living the life you had, and the life you have access to today.

Love,

Dad

The two dozen photos in the journal stretched over her 20 years, capturing family, friends, trips, parties, and simple things. The pictures included: Rose at two years old in a one-piece sleeper; three sisters in the bathtub—two, five, and eight years old; her third birthday party at Chuck E. Cheese; the family loaded in the Volvo wagon on a trip with Mom; the family all dressed in white shirts at the beach; her ten-year-old birthday party; her sister's high school graduation; her sixteenth birthday; her first day with a driver's license; Dad and Rose with blue wigs on at UNC basketball game; Rose on her first day of school in first and twelfth grade; the family at Thanksgiving; Rose with her freshman year sorority sisters; and Rose in front of Breakaway Rehab facility (#29).

I was hopeful many, many times.

Rose,

I hope you look at these photos and remember the good times we've had—and can still have. It is up to you to take responsibility for yourself. While I do not fully understand addiction, I know you must face it, figure a path to a healthier life, and get clean, so you can move on with your life. I know it is not that simple or easy.

It has taken us four years to understand how addiction is affecting you, and we wish you would:

- Reconnect with your family, rebuilding the relationships and lost trust
- Build a plan to minimize the risk of drug use and dishonesty
- Support yourself
- Seek out happiness
- Believe in your heart that you deserve a beautiful life

We love you, but do not like your choices.

Much Love,

Dad

I gave her the photo journal sitting in a car parking lot in front of a telephone store where we were getting her phone password reset. In a paranoid moment the day before she changed it and could not remember what the password was. It was emotional and uplifting for me putting the photo journal together. She was outwardly surprised by the thought of me digging through pictures, pasting them into a book and writing notes around the pictures. She looked at each picture recalling a detail or two that I had forgotten. She started to cry.

"I don't deserve a good life because of the things I have done," she said.

It made me sad as I vociferously tried to explain why she does deserve a good life—we all do. There is always forgiveness, revival, renewal, rejuvenation, transformation… it fell on quiet ears.

She still carries the photo journal around and mentions it, a small victory.

CHAPTER XXIX

Enduring Legacy

I SOMETIMES CAN'T BELIEVE it's been a decade since that first phone call, that life-changing event. It seems I did not start appreciating time on this planet until after that wake-up call. Before I awoke, time was something that I managed, or it managed me. I marched to the beat of the calendar; it was a routine, just what everyone else did. After Lisa was diagnosed, I came to understand that we all walk through life carrying the traits and experiences from our family and prior generations. Acknowledging that provides introspection, and helps me to focus on the good with new awareness. The legacy of the last ten years since my life-changing experience is that I have come to think a bit differently. Now I would say:

- Be your true self
- Trust yourself and your cumulative experiences
- You deserve a full and good life
- Do not let anyone put you in a box that they get to define
- Know you did the best you could at the time
- Acknowledge that hindsight will be superior like a backseat driver
- Know that there will be good days and bad
- Live through the bad to get to the good; they're coming, I promise

- Focus on your true friends and positive relationships
- Find what this new life entails for you, and don't be afraid to seek it out
- Learn from the past, dream about the future, and live in the present
- Live

But what about the Enduring Legacy or the Unintended Legacy? That is, how are the girls like their mom?

Remember that Mother's Day when I was trying not to cry in the middle of church? While I thought of it then, I want to share it with you now for better context. That Mother's Day experience made me think of one of my favorite movies, *The Lion King*. It is a great movie in many respects. One of the most powerful lines in the story is when Rafiki tells Simba, "He lives in you," when discussing the death of Mufasa, Simba's father. It is one of the most relevant and overlooked stories about generational legacy and processing grief. The heartwarming message is that who we become is significantly influenced by our parents. It is our connection to past and future generations.

The little things we do every day as parents builds an enduring legacy in our children. And so it is with my girls. In many respects, it is an accidental legacy built out of necessity, or things that their mom and I enjoyed. The girls laugh as they talk about the fun things we did together that really stuck with them throughout their adult lives, such as cooking, growing a garden, building things with wood, playing tennis, reading books, and playing outdoors.

Each one of them shares characteristics with their mom. If you drew out behavioral continuums, each girl would fall into a different place based on the characteristic described, some of the girls being more like me, and some of them being more like their mother. I would have it no other way.

But on that first Mother's Day alone I was asking myself, *What is their mom's enduring legacy with our children? What do I see of Lisa in each girl?* It did not take me long, as it is easy to see her in each of them.

Charlotte shows her mom's gracious and welcoming nature, always ready to open up and engage anyone on any topic, making everyone feel welcomed in the process. She displays a kind and caring nature, and wants to make a difference in people's lives; many of her friends seek her counsel and advice. Like her mom, she is the firstborn and a rule-follower. They also share the desire to plan events for all occasions and make everyday events something special. Nothing about life is going to be average when they're in charge.

June has her mom's zest for life, as well as her quick wit, and is up for margaritas and Mexican food anytime. She has her mom's boisterous laugh, with the same tone and cadence that allows her to fit seamlessly into any situation. June has a big heart and is willing to share it freely with friends and strangers alike. She also has her mom's love for animals (even though Lisa was allergic to cats, we had two, a dog and a rabbit).

Rose has her mom's smile; she can light up any room with her easygoing demeanor and bright, magnetic eyes. Like her mom, she is very positive, nor does she stay mad long. Everyone likes her and is drawn to her. Just like Lisa, she is off-the-charts smart and athletic, especially in tennis. I will never forget helping Rose with her math homework in the fourth grade; she found the answer right away, and when I asked her to show me her work, she said, "Dad, I just get math!" She's right, she really does.

Each girl carries an enduring, individual legacy from their mom. No one can change or dispute that. A common characteristic that they all carry from Lisa is that they are attractive in a warm way, welcoming, and encouraging to all.

The thought made me happy.

Summary Thoughts for a Family in the Storm of Grief

A LIFE-CHANGING EVENT IS JUST THAT—LIFE-CHANGING.
Throughout the last ten years life has changed significantly for my family and will continue to evolve. Each of our individual and combined perceptions about what and how things happened and felt, have with time changed a bit over that ten-year period. Condensing the real-time thoughts and prospective thoughts throughout the book with the benefit of ten years of reflection yielded this epilogue.

These ideas and suggestions may be helpful for both grievers and friends of grievers. Feel free to use and share these distilled thoughts as guidance or support for anyone who has experienced a loss. This summary of key elements of experiences and thoughts are grouped into the categories of **The Griever, The Grieving Family,** and **Friends and Relatives of a Grieving Family** for quick review and thought.

ooooo

THE GRIEVER

Before the life changing event:

- If it is not too late, clear the deck every day with your spouse so if something happens you do not spend any time voicing regrets. It is also a more wholesome spousal relationship.
- Embrace quiet thought alone. Listen to what comes to mind.
- The minute you are aware of a life-threatening healthcare situation, identify a family member or friend who can help you or be your healthcare advocate to navigate the amount of information coming at you fast and prioritize the decisions to be made.
- When the time comes, step up prepared to be present and follow your intuition.
- Identify one friend or relative who can act as your connection and communicator to your friends. Everyone will want to speak directly with you, and it is important to speak with everyone at least once. After that you may not have the emotional or physical energy to field calls or emails. Friends will understand when your identified person calls them back and explains. It also helps the caller to know they can call someone for updates without burdening the griever.
- Be honest with your children, omitting some of the granular, gory details. Tell them what you do and do not know.
- Even if you promised to tell a loved one the absolute truth about an illness, weigh that promise and truth from the context of new information. Consider the current state of health and time remaining of the one who is ill. There is no wrong decision.
- Consider what would help the dying patient best in this most undefined transition.
- Physicians currently frame the question of further treatment for cancer patients in the most impossible and contorted way… The question is not *Are you going to fight this or give in?* The question to the doctor is, *What is your best estimate of how long I will live with good quality of life based on all of your experience and current research available?*

- The question for the patient is, *Given the estimated time I have left in this world how do I want to spend it?* Would I prefer two good months without chemotherapy, or the chance for six months slowly being killed by the poison of chemotherapy or radio therapy? Again, there is no wrong choice.
- What quality of life do I want for that window of time?
- Knowing what I know, living what I lived, I would not choose current cancer therapy for myself unless there was a strong indication of extending my life by 12 months or more. The State of the Art Oncology in many cases is overstated when compared to the Quality of Life remaining.

After the life-changing event:

- Your life will never be the same. The instant it changed, it changed forever. You must start to process the change, accept some part of it and start reconciling the rest of your life plan.
- Be present, today. Do not seek to rush or slow the speed of your grief. Mindfully start to be aware of its evolution and its fluctuations between what might seem to be too much and too little. It is okay to smile and laugh again on any day. You are not being disrespectful—be happy.
- Grief timing and processing are on *your* clock and schedule, but you do not have full control of that schedule.
- Grief triggers—the details of past life experiences and emotions that tend to plunge you into sadness or deep sorrow—can show up at any point without warning.
- Grief triggers are real, intense rushes of emotion and can be rescripted in a fashion to celebrate the person you are missing versus making you feel guilty.
- Grief triggers are external, emotionally charged hypersensitivities that teleport your mind to another place time and event. People, smells, pictures, music, noise, animals, and other things that stimulate a vivid memory of your lost loved one.
- Grief triggers quietly ambush you at the most inopportune times.

- Know there will be good days and bad, that there is hope and the future is bright.
- When thinking about future memories and legacy, ask yourself: *What tangible "things" might your family benefit from in ten years?*
- Write your own eulogy and share it with no one. Begin it with, *I did the best I could with what I had at the time.*
- The deceased does not belong on a pedestal or a cross; treat them as they were in your life—an integral part of everyday living.
- Acknowledge that today is a low point in your life and tomorrow is another day.
- On the day of passing, acknowledge to yourself that your new life starts tomorrow morning.
- Fear and anxiety will be powerful adversaries when you worry about your children.
- You cannot know all, just trust you have done the best job you could do.
- Acknowledge these intense emotions and embrace them as a celebration of the spirit of the one you lost. It is not only okay; it is therapeutic or cathartic.
- Recognize that friends are going to inadvertently create some of these triggers.
- Unrelated things will remind you at inopportune times of what has happened.
- Some friends do unusually inappropriate things because of their personal unprocessed issues and the personal rewards they seek. It is not about you; it is about them. Do not sweat it.
- Denial is not a plan.
- Write a journal of your feelings and thoughts. It is liberating and truly cathartic.
- Seek out who you are and who you want to be.
- Relinquishing the driving, controlling instinct demonstrates that you have faith in yourself.
- What you say to people puts your words out to the Universe and strikes your destiny. Think about what you say.

- Listen and come to know everyone's mental and physical limits, which will inform the necessity of an intervention.
- Take a deep breath and say to others, "I will think about what you said."

THE GRIEVING FAMILY

- It is impossible to prepare for all of the situations and comments that the grieving family will encounter.
- Trauma is an event. Grief is a mechanism to process the traumatic event.
- Grief affects people outside of the family life for only an hour or so a week; it affects the direct family every minute, and for the rest of their lives. Recognize and respect that grief is a new piece of clothing that you wear 24 hours a day everyday.
- Emotions of grief will ebb and flow over the years for a motherless daughter.
- All in the family should say out loud that there is hope and the future is bright.
- Seek out and identify your successful grieving coping mechanisms such as quiet time for yourself, a hobby, a distraction such as a crossword puzzle, exercise, and others.
- Recurring themes for the grieving family include: Trust, trust, trust your intuition. Be honest with your children and close friends about how you feel. Believe in your judgment, what your heart and soul are saying to you. Feel the moment; live in the present.
- There is no going back, once change has entered your life in this way.
- Hope is at the heart of an optimistic outlook and is key to recovery from a grief wound, even for children.
- No matter how involved a parent you are, you may not know your children as well as you think you do. Check in with them and do not make assumptions based on your thoughts; ask them.
- Tell family members what you know and what you do not know at the time it is happening, because they already know something is up.

Children will hold you accountable for what you tell them that may turn out to be incorrect. Be aware and over communicate or review with them to optimize clarity.

- It is important to give children information in bites that they can understand.
- In communicating with children, keep the facts consistent and together, while acknowledging your feelings and suggest the children share feelings with you and each other.
- Your life can change in an instant is not just a cliché.
- Go to therapy. Talk therapy is helpful today and tomorrow.
- Require all family directly touched by grief to have at least five sessions with a therapist.
- Encourage your therapist to teach tools to handle situations that family members encounter; they will know. Simple things such as learning how to catch yourself sinking into negative ruminations and positive ways to change the direction of thinking will save you significant energy and improve your stamina.
- Know that the person, the spirit, and the role will be missed throughout your lifetime.
- Choose to be happy, because you can. I have.
- Children of different ages have different feelings based on their experiences, birth order, and age when the traumatic event occurred.
- Parents, do not allow a child of any age to assume the parenting role. My oldest unknowingly tried to assume a different role which seemed to evaporate her childhood and over the years could lead to resentment of innocence and childhood prematurely taken away. As a child of trauma, children must be and act their age in this type of disaster.
- After a few weeks our family did not want others to see them crying, but it is okay to cry in public and with your family. No matter how you plan or prepare not to cry or let things get to you, some things will pop up and shock you. It is okay.
- The monster called Fear and Uncertainty prevails in young children's minds embroiled in a traumatic event. Just as a child might put a pretend monster in the closet in their room, it is important to teach

them how to take the monster out of the dark and expose it to the light.

- It seems that younger children do not clearly understand what is happening in this very traumatic environment. Children have very real fears and concerns about the basic things in life, focusing on unusual things, many driven by fear. Adults, acknowledge and pay attention to these very real emotions. Take them seriously. There will be questions, voiced or not, logical or not, such as: *Who will take care of me? What will happen to my things in my room? Who will get them? Where will I go? What is next?* Some variation on these questions are in all young children's minds. Be aware and help them understand as many answers as possible and minimize the anxiety around the questions that they cannot answer. If uncertainty prevails, be as truthful as possible and provide some plan or time frame for resolution. Children in trauma need a warm security blanket.

- Parents, do not blame or shame yourself, because you did the best you could at the time with what you had. Say that out loud to show for your children, often, along with how proud of them you are.

- Be frank but not blunt, direct but not cutting, in consideration of fragile family feelings.

- Grief is a powerful emotion, worthy of leading, driving, and empowering a positive contribution to the rest of your life—*or* it can be draining, depleting, and lead to a dismal free fall into negative, destructive emotions. As an adult you understand that you control your destiny; children may not know how to handle the emotional challenge of balancing positive and negative emotions. Set healthy boundaries for processing grief.

- Focus as much as possible on what your family *does* have.

- Daily positive affirmations help with the low periods. Yellow sticky notes spread around the house really help. The notes are unique to you and your children. Pick fun thoughts for the kids such as labeling *ice cream Wednesday after dinner, movie night, pizza night, puzzle night,* or other fun things the family likes to do together. For adults it may be a smiley face on a sticky note by your bed, or *I am appreciated* by your toothbrush, or *I am a great parent to my children* by your mirror.

- Find little things that help you get through the first few months, puzzles, hobbies, walking, reading—anything, particularly if you can do it together as a family.
- Acknowledge that just keeping it together is hard.
- Refocus on the philosophy of faith regardless of your religion. It gets you through many of the down times and heightens to good times together with the family.
- Grief exposes unresolved issues in everyone.
- Processing grief will require visiting and starting to resolve, at least in part, any issues that have not been settled.
- My experience is that the shock of the girls of losing their mom at nine, twelve, and fifteen years old carried a great burden, that can amount to P T S D (post-traumatic stress disorder). Treat it as such.
- Avoidance is not a grief or loss coping skill.
- Well-meaning people will do and say things that will make you angry.
- It is okay to be frustrated, anxious, and angry. Lashing out at others is not okay.
- Focusing on being present and mindful will help you more than any drug.
- Consider asking a physician about short-term use of antidepressants for situational grief. It can add about 20 percent more padding under your carpet for the daily excruciating mental pain inflicted on you by the sudden situation. It is not weak or shameful to draw on this resource.
- If you choose not to consider a few months of antidepressants and are going at it alone, be aware that self-medication with alcohol can become a crutch and risk.
- Grief does not follow the tidy five-step process of Denial, Anger, Bargaining, Depression, and Acceptance.
- Grief is a uniquely individual and highly emotional, messy process that resembles an overlapping series of Venn diagrams (see page 83).

- Talk with your children to prepare them for the awkwardness of talking with their friends. They likely will not fully understand in advance, but some preparation is better than none.
- Provide your young grievers with words to help them understand that their friends are trying their best to show kindness, offer friendship, and be helpful. Equip children with a statement to respond to an unexpected question or a statement to use in their peer groups. It reduces anxiety.
- Stressful times do not build character—they bring it out.
- True friends will support and help you; let the rest be.
- Most of your friends will be helpful in thought, word, and deed. Focus on them.
- There is no antidote for judgment and hypocrisy, only tolerance.
- Hitting back at someone who says the wrong thing or an eye for an eye is not helpful; just put it in a mental parking lot. Give it a number. Mine is Parking Lot #3. It is full of rusty vehicles from people who have unprocessed conflict and issues that impede their true abilities and senses.
- Do not be surprised when some of your friends do not support your thoughts, statements, or actions. They are at a very different stage of grief.
- Listen closely and engage with the friends who are positive and supportive.
- Healthy spousal relationships carry an exuberance and unmatched successful feeling. Bereaved partners who have had successful and healthy spousal relationships can be ready for a new relationship almost immediately. But of course, only the healthiest know.
- Making a link between a traumatic event in a child's younger life and a behavioral or emotional result later in life may be helpful to inform treatment.
- It is not your fault; you did nothing wrong.
- I have always talked with the girls about the consequences of their actions, good and bad, but had no understanding as to the magnitude of pain that unresolved grief could inflict.

- Significant parallels exist between grief, loss, and addiction recovery. Addiction may also be a way to avoid grief or feel better about it.

- Being connected to friends, community, your tribe, golf buddies, soft ball team, Rotary Club, girls wine club, Bunko groups, and any other group of friends sharing commonality is what makes society work.

- Seek out meaningful connections to communities.

- Invest in reconnecting.

- Children of all ages remember, rewrite, and rescript history as you know it. It is okay if they are wrong! Remind children how you remember what happened in a light and happy way.

- Children will likely not fully appreciate how much you have done until they have children. It is okay.

- Remind children that even under duress of the situation, that you all had a great journey, and the adventure is not over.

- As my daughters grew into a young adults, they tried to remember more of the good times that we learned from rather than the hard experiences that scarred us.

- This experience may make my daughters more engaged, better mothers.

- Children under ten years of age will likely struggle the most with understanding and grieving in the near and longer term.

- Acknowledging children's feelings and emotions is important at the moment a troubling incident occurs. Acknowledgment validates and supports children and adults struggling for context of the new normal of their life.

FRIENDS AND RELATIVES OF THE GRIEVING FAMILY

- It is the little things that help grievers.

- The greatest gift you could give a grieving friend or relative is the gift of graciousness; that is, provide your friend with heaping amounts of unselfish, understanding, tolerance, sensitivity, and kindness. Give it freely.

- Reread the questions in Chapter 22 before talking to a friend in grief.

- Think of life from the griever's perspective.
- Grace is about a position; gratitude is about the giver, but graciousness is the greatest gift.
- Good friends of all ages could say what my twelve-year-old's friend said to her: "I do not know what to say, but when you want to talk, I will be here to talk with you." It is that simple, because it lets them know they have a safe place to go and a known friend to go with.

HOSPICE

- Hospice is a wonderful, kind, and gentle service valuable to the patient and the family members that is available in your own home. Please draw on this resource. Most insurance covers this service.
- Death is a transition for the traveler. Hospice helped me to understand that each person's transition is different. Embrace the uniqueness of the transition as a wonder of life.
- Talk with hospice and listen. Embrace hospice services as they prepare everyone in your home for what is happening before it happens.

OTHER RELATED THOUGHTS

- Since inception in 1971, the war on drugs has cost US taxpayers more than 950 billion dollars, while the goverment has reduced spending on mental health and increased the public shame, guilt, and prevalence of drug use in America. In 2018, 35,000 of the annual 70,000 opioid overdose deaths were physician-prescribed opioids. Over a ten-year period 57,939 soldiers died in Vietnam.
- Since inception in 1971, the war on cancer has cost US taxpayers more than 500 billion dollars and contributed significantly to increased healthcare costs. Advances have been debated.

Acknowledgements

I AM GRATEFUL TO my three sweet daughters for their willingness to expose the most private of thoughts in this expression of love. Thank you, Susanna for not living in the shadow, but casting your own. Thank you to my family for embracing my fierce passion for life.

This project would not likely have seen sunlight without Clyde Edgerton's wisdom, encouragement and advice. I am deeply appreciative for the encouragement to look around the corner.

Thank you, Peggy Payne for putting the pieces of the puzzle in the right order, Diana Clark for polishing them, and Katie Prince for transforming the words into images.

And to all of my great friends...you know who you are.

Made in the USA
Columbia, SC
10 August 2020